Other works by Carl Reiner:

Enter Laughing

The 2000 Year Old Man:
The Complete History

All Kinds of Love

Continue Laughing

The 2000 Year Old Man in
the Year 2000: The Book

How Paul Robeson Saved My Life
And Other Mostly Happy Stories

My Anecdotal Life

NNNNN

Just Desserts: A Novellelah

I Remember Me

Children's books by Carl Reiner:

Tell Me A Scary Story
But Not Too Scary!

The 2000 Year Old Man
Goes To School

Tell Me Another Scary Story
But Not Too Scary!

Tell Me A Silly Story

Too Scared To Scream

The Secret Treasure Of Kahka Paka

I
Just
Remembered

Carl Reiner

RANDOM
CONTENT
PUBLISHING

RANDOM CONTENT™
Beverly Hills, CA 90210
www.randomcontent.com

Published by RANDOM CONTENT 04/22/14

ISBN: 978-0-9915367-0-2

Library of Congress Control Number: 2014936714

Front cover photo by Unknown
Back cover photo by Unknown

Any people depicted in images have given approval by their estate and trustees.

This book is printed on acid-free paper.

Because of the dynamic nature of the Internet, any web addresses
or links contained in this book may have changed since publication
and may no longer be valid.

Cpl. Carl Reiner in "Shape Ahoy" 1944

"Inviting people to laugh at you when you are laughing at yourself is a good thing to do. You may be the fool but you're the fool in charge."

Carl Reiner–My Anecdotal Life*

Carl Reiner as Al Schilling in "The Comic"

Contents

CHAPTER 1   I Just Remembered I Had Forgotten H. V. Kaltenborn   1

CHAPTER 2   On Awakening This Morning I Jotted Down MBr -MBr   7

CHAPTER 3   Ira Wolfer's Untimely Erection   19

CHAPTER 4   The Corporal, The Con Man And The Chupah Pole   25

CHAPTER 5   Teaching Joyce Kuntz to Pronounce Her Name Correctly   37

CHAPTER 6   Three Operatic Tenors, Two I Owe and One Owes Me   43

CHAPTER 7   Jack Paar Tells Tales of Castro, Cuba and Castration   53

CHAPTER 8   The Once Tarnished Golden Globes   61

CHAPTER 9   Get Behind That Big Wooden Crate And Don't Move!   67

CHAPTER 10   The Mystery Of The Gold Money Clip and The Rubber Band   73

CHAPTER 11   The Most Self-Involved Friend I Have   83

CHAPTER 12   The Poor Peddler and The Carefree Colt   91

CHAPTER 13   Ah The Sweet Unsolved Mysteries Of My Life   99

CHAPTER 14   How, In Just Thirty Days, I Learned All The Lyrics
To A Very Short Song   107

CHAPTER 15   To Pass Time Faster I Sing My Arias Slower   113

CHAPTER 16   47 Real Appearances with Johnny Carson and 3 Fake Ones   119

CHAPTER 17   This Here Book... By Cark Reimer   122

CHAPTER 18   Shakespeare Misspoke, The Play Is Not The Thing,
The Audience Is The Thing!   141

CHAPTER 19   How I Learned 'YouTube' Is Not 'HisTube,' 'HerTube,' 'YourTube,' 'Their Tube,' Or 'Anybody Else In The Entire World's Tube,' But 'My Tube,'   147

CHAPTER 20   How To Wisely Use The Hairs On Your Balding Head   153

CHAPTER 21   Tom Bergeron And My Old Hot Dog Dilemma   159

CHAPTER 22   I Just Re-Remembered Laramie Lois   165

CHAPTER 23   Oh For The Days Of Yore   171

CHAPTER 24   Treat Your Feet Right And Your Toes Will Thank You   177

CHAPTER 25   Checkups Can Allay Checkouts   183

CHAPTER 26   Reiner Record Residual   189

CHAPTER 27   A Treasure Trove Of An Elderly Gent's Daily Tweets   195

CHAPTER 28   The Ten Telltale Signs Of My Encroaching Expiration Date   207

CHAPTER 29   I Thank You Papa For The Good Advice And The Good Genes   215

CHAPTER 30   Why Mel B. And I Knew The Answer to The 1st Question On "Jeopardy"   223

CHAPTER 31   Measuring The True Length Of A Modern Marriage   233

CHAPTER 32   One Must Be 100% Alive to Write About Death   239

CHAPTER 33   The Very Last One After The One Purporting To Be The Last One or Once Again I Invoke Columbo's "Uh, Just One More Thing"   243

CHAPTER 34   Instead Of Starting An Extremely Short New Bio, I Am Adding This…   249

CHAPTER 35   Oooh, I Just Remembered What I Almost Forgot   255

Photo Index   322

When asked of which theatrical project I'm most proud,
I answer, "Creating the Dick Van Dyke Show, hands down."

From left to right: Lucas Reiner, Maude Reiner, Ann Winchester, Livia Reiner, GordonWinchester, Nicole Silberkleit, Sonja Hansen, Michele Reiner, Romy Reiner, Rob Reiner, President Clinton, Ilse Reiner, Elaine Reiner, Carl & Estelle Reiner, Annie Reiner, Richard Reiner and Helene Reiner. In front center: Nick Reiner, Jake Reiner & Charles Reiner.

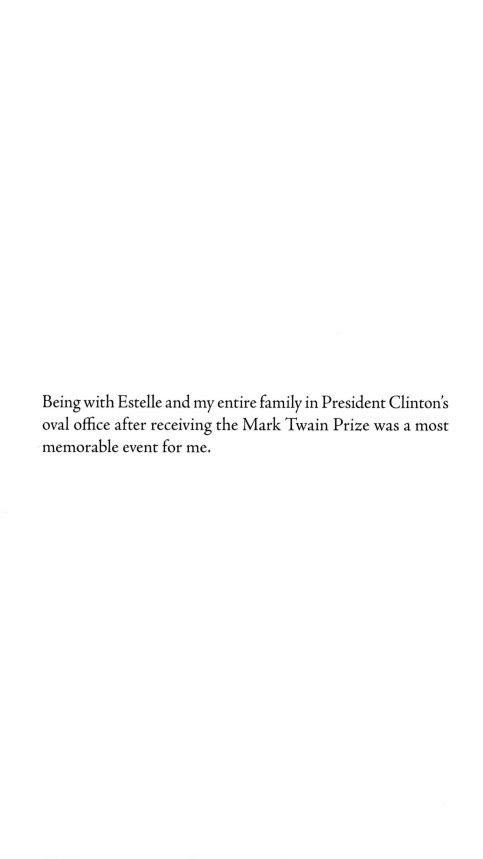

Being with Estelle and my entire family in President Clinton's oval office after receiving the Mark Twain Prize was a most memorable event for me.

Foreword

Carl Reiner's mind takes you through time and space like the Starship Enterprise. He knows about living, having lived and the will to live. Like most comedians I know, 99% of his brain is consumed by either a joke, a pretty girl or what to eat. With the 1% that remained, Carl fought a war, raised a family and had one of the most spectacular show business careers anyone has ever seen. And he remembers every day of it. With this wonderful new book we get to remember it along with him including bountiful buttocks, departing follicles and inopportune erections. I love that Carl is still riding life like a roller coaster and giving us a seat right next to him.

–Jerry Seinfeld
New York City

Preface

One morning, a week after I was informed that "I Remember Me" was being published, I awoke with two memories: a game called "Reallies" that my pal Mel Brooks and I invented in 1950, and the other involved Jack Paar and a journalist, H. V. Kaltenborn. I would have included both stories in my biography had I remembered them in time. For the next few months, every time I went for my morning stroll, some distant memory would flood back. I felt that some were worthy of being catalogued, and thereupon, "I Just Remembered..." was born.

Acknowledgement

My heartfelt thanks to: first my family, Rob, Annie, Lucas, my grandchildren Jake, Nick, Romy, Livia, Rose and my daughters-in-law Michele and Maud.

And Bess Scher, George Shapiro and Al Pivo.

My deep gratitude to the publishers @RandomContent Lawrence O'Flahavan and Aaron Davis for their friendship and their diligence in digging into cartons of old photos from which they selected images that chronicled my life in 'Show Biz.' They then edited those down to two-hundred-and-twenty-six photographs that make up this autobiography, photos that will take you back to the days of yore.*

* For more of "the days of yore", see Chapter 22.

H. V. Kaltenborn, News Analyst 1939

I Just Remembered I Had Completely Forgotten
H.V. Kaltenborn

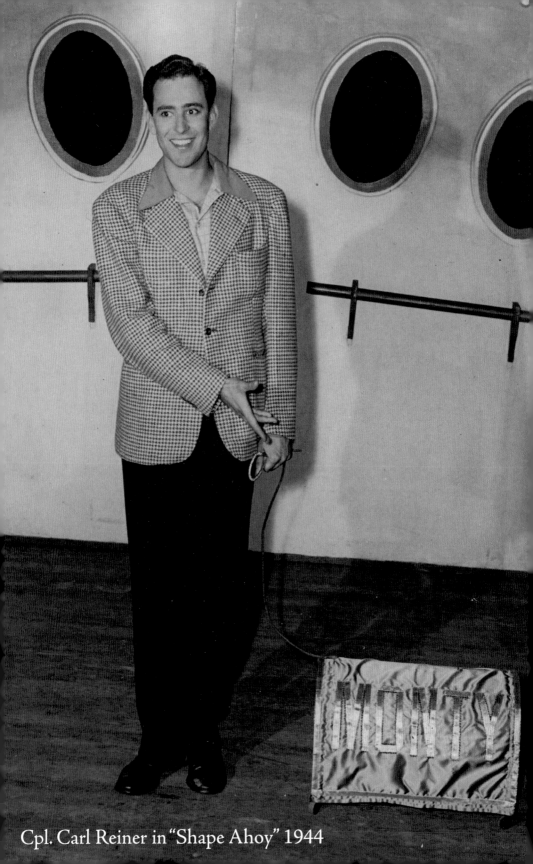

Cpl. Carl Reiner in "Shape Ahoy" 1944

I Just Remembered I Had Completely Forgotten H.V. Kaltenborn

Just three mornings ago, on awakening, I jotted down: HV Ka and deemed it worthy of a short chapter. I trust I have deemed correctly. The HV Ka I noted was to remind myself of a dream I had in which H.V. Kaltenborn appeared. H. V. Kaltenborn was a popular newspaper journalist of the nineteen twenties and thirties, who became a fixture on radio and television. Mr. Kaltenborn started his illustrious radio career in 1928 on CBS and soon left to join NBC, where he remained for thirty years. He is credited with being the first broadcaster to analyze the news. At six o'clock, every weekday evening, my father tuned in to hear Mr. Kaltenborn comment on our nation's problems. I was about twelve when I first took note of him. I was not at all interested in what he was saying but tickled by the way he was saying it. I was intrigued by the strange, singsong, staccato cadence to his delivery. It was easy to mimic, so I did.

H.V. was the first of many impressions I did of famous people. During my stint in the Army, I entertained our troops illustrating how my deceased pet, "Monty The Talking Dog," was capable of doing "spot-on" impersonations of such film stars as Ronald Colman, Charles Boyer, Jimmy Stewart and Akim Tamiroff.

Ronald Colman Jimmy Stewart Charles Boyer Akim Tamirof

Adolf Hitler 1938

As I was saying before interrupting myself to explain who H.V. was, in my dream it seemed that HV and I had a short exchange about Adolph Hitler, German Shepard dogs and Jews. I thought it occurred on Jack Paar's late night talk show. In striving for accuracy, I Googled the "Jack Paar Show" and discovered that in 1960-61 both Kaltenborn and myself had been booked as guests but not on the same shows.

I remember Kaltenborn, during one of his appearances with Jack, talking about a trip he had made to the Bavarian Alps in 1938. He had arranged to interview the Fuhrer, at a magnificent chateau in Berchtesgarden. He described their meeting and how much he detested this horrible man. He spoke of how Hitler's face lit up when his two dogs romped out to greet him.

I remember too, seeing film of der Fuhrer bending over and lovingly petting the frisky animals, as a narrator's voice commented that "The Fuhrer who was capable of having a warm relationship with animals was a side of Hitler that few people ever knew."

"How about the side of Hitler," I shouted at the TV set, **"when he killed six million Jews? They sure must've known about that! Hitler made sure they did and he boasted about it to the world! The sonofabitch Nazi Bastard!"**

Tonight I hope I dream of June Allison...

June Allison

Marlon Brando

On Awakening This Morning I Jotted Down MBr-MBr

Mel Brooks -1953

CHAPTER TWO

On Awakening This Morning I Jotted Down MBr-MBr

Since I so enjoyed writing Chapter One based on my jotting down 'H V Ka' which reminded me of my truck with H.V. Kaltenborn, I was happy this morning to see these letters 'MBr-MBr' that I had written on my bedside pad. If you guessed that the letters stood for two memories of **Mel Brooks**, then you would be half right and you would be one hundred percent correct if you guessed that the second 'MBr' stood for another show biz icon, **Marlon Brando** .

I will deal first with Marlon, whose acquaintance I made in 1947. It was in Boston when I was starring in the road company of Harold Rome's musical revue, "Call Me Mister," and Marlon was starring with Tallulah Bankhead in Jean Cocteau's "The Eagle Has Two Heads."

I remember my first meeting him when he came into my dressing room at the Shubert Theater, introduced himself and went on to praise my performance. At the time, his play was in rehearsal and set to open in a week. He invited our whole cast to attend a pre-opening preview and, to this day, I remember the incredibly positive impression he made. He gave a revelatory performance that night, in the sense that we saw and heard a Brando that, in later years, no one knew existed those years in which he portrayed the mumbling, inarticulate slob, Stanley Kowalski so brilliantly in Tennessee Williams' "A Street Car Named Desire". The world thought that that was Marlon Brando, but when called upon the 'real Brando' was capable of delivering speeches that were soaring and well enunciated. At Boston's Colonial Theater, thanks to Jean Cocteau, I heard Marlon Brando speak a speech, as Shakespeare put it, "trippingly on the tongue." In years to come, Marlon displayed the depth of his vocal and acting talents in such roles as, Marc Anthony in "Julius Caesar," Fletcher Christian in "Mutiny On The Bounty" and Vito Corleone in "The Godfather."

That day in Boston, during a period when Marlon was not in rehearsal, he sat in my dressing room waiting for the curtain to come down on our show's finale. The first time Marlon saw "Call Me Mister," his eye was caught by a comely, redheaded, chorus dancer, Nina Starkey. I believe that their relationship was as short-lived as Cocteau's play and Brando's stay in Boston.

One thing I will never forget was a question that Marlon posed that I thought strange, coming from a man who really knew his way about a stage. He asked me how, when I was singing this number, as a member of a trio, I got my eyes to sparkle so effectively. He sounded genuinely impressed as he described his sitting in the balcony and marveling at my ability to make my "eyes flash like that." I told him that all I was doing was singing to the audience. When we favored the audience on the main floor, my eyes were looking down but when I looked up to the balcony, I naturally opened them wider and the spotlights simply bounced off the whites of my eyes, without me doing one thing special.

I am now ready to deal with the other MBr I jotted on my bedside note pad. It pertained to detailed conversations that Mel Brooks and I had started over sixty years ago. In the course of these chats, we entertained each other by discussing, in depth, and with a studied sincerity, a variety of mundane subjects. We call these inane discussions "Reallies". A "Reallie" can be inspired by almost anything, a TV drama, a live baseball game or an advertising slogan.

If memory serves me, and so far it has-- Mel and I had our first "Reallie" exchange when we worked on "Your Show Of Shows." Sid Caesar was a serious cigar smoker, as were many of the members of the writing staff. Those were the good old days when sophisticated smokers heeded the advice of their tobacconists rather than their doctors.

Sid, being the show's top banana, smoked a cigar that resembled a banana, an imported Cuban #1 Montecristo, as did our head writer, Mel Tolkin, whom Sid kept supplied. Lucille Kallen, Joe Stein and Mel Brooks smoked a version of a cigar that came into being at the turn of the century, commonly called a cigarette, and Neil (Doc) Simon was too young to smoke.

I had not been a smoker when I signed on as Sid's straight man, but after a six-hour day in the writers' room, I smelled like a smoker. My wife, Estelle told me this after stepping back from a 'welcome-home-from-work'-embrace. It was then I decided that if I was going to smell like a cigar smoker, I might as well be one and join the club.

Now, what kind of cigar would suit me? I saw myself not as a business mogul, but as a suave, riverboat gambler named Gaylord something, so the cigar that best fit that image was a long, thin Panatela.

Mel and I started our first "Reallie" in Max's office after I had removed the paper cigar band from one of my Panatelas and dropped it into the ashtray beside Mel Brooks' chair. As you may or may not know, a serious cigar smoker never, ever smoked a cigar that still had its band in place. It was just not done.

As I sat down across the room, Mel picked my cigar band from the ashtray, put it on his pinky finger, raised his hand, and asked:

"Carl, what do you think?"

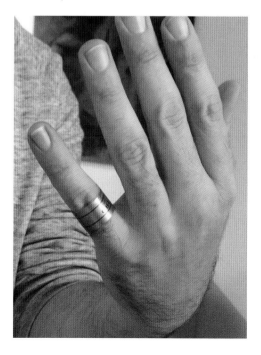

I looked, thought a moment and said, "It's beautiful!"

"Do you really like it?" Mel asked, coyly.

"Yes, very much, it's a winner. When did you get it?"

"This morning." Mel answered, modeling it.

"You got good taste, Mel. Where did you get it, Tiffany?"

"No, from this ash tray, where you dropped it."

"C'mon," I said, in disbelief, "that's not my...?"

"Yes it is!" he laughed. "It's the band you took off your cigar."

"I don't believe it," I said, squinting. "It looks like a real gold ring!"

"Well, it's a real paper ring." Mel said, modeling it.

"You sneak, you switched it with a real gold one, didn't you?"

"I did not!" Mel said, handing it to me. "See for yourself."

"I'll be darned! Mel, from five feet away, it looked like a 14 karat beaut."

As Mel returned to his seat, I put the cigar band on my finger.

"Look," I said, flashing it, "doesn't it look like real gold?"

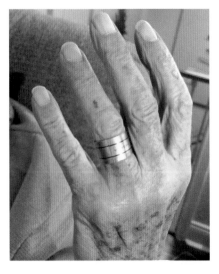

"You sonofagun," he laughed, "Where the hell did you get that?"

"From you, who took it from that ashtray where I put it."

"Carl, you put a paper cigar band in the ashtray and what you're flashing is no paper cigar band. That baby is at least 14, maybe 18 karat gold!"

"Well, if it is 18 karats, you're in luck, Mel," I said, taking the paper cigar band from my finger, "because I am giving it to you as a birthday present."

"My birthday isn't till June," he said, taking the cigar band, "and I can't accept such an expensive ring."

"Sure you can, take it Mel."

"Hey, this is the cigar band, what did you do with the gold one?"

"There is no gold one!" I yelled.

"You slipped it into your pocket and pulled out this paper one. Empty your pocket!"

"Mel, I do not have a gold ring in my pocket. I say wherever it is, we sell it and share the loot—fifty-fifty."

"How about sixty-sixty?"

"Even better!"

Carl Reiner & Mel Brooks 1951

The following is a current "Reallie" that Mel and I had just a few nights ago while watching television. An ad came on promoting a new motion picture and after informing us how entertaining the film was, the announcer added: "Playing everywhere, this Friday."

"Hey Carl, the man said that movie, is playing everywhere."
"That's great, Mel! We could go see it at the Landmark Theater."
"Across town? Carl, we'd have to drive there."
"Where would you like to see it?"
"Well, he said it's playing everywhere. How about Dr. Ahnsue's office? I've got a dental appointment at three."
"Mel, isn't his office rather small?"
"It is... Hey, we could see it at Whole Foods on Crescent Drive, it's only three blocks away."
"Rite Aid is two blocks away and less crowded."
"Nate 'n Al's is even closer, and Carl we can pick up some corned beef sandwiches."
"Wait, they deliver! I'll call them."
"Carl, you're a genius! My treat!"
"Over my dead body!"
"As you wish!"

A "Reallie" always works well when watching a TV show.
Here is an example of a "Reallie" when we watched a Police drama:

"Mel, why did that cop get into that car when he knew it was going to blow up?"
"Because, Carl, he didn't know."
"How could he not know?"
"How could he know?"
"Mel, he read the darn script, didn't he?"
"Of course, that's why he got into the car. He'd read the directions."
"Right, and the directions must have also said, 'car explodes'!"
"So?"
"So? Mel, he could have refused—why didn't he?"
"Because he would have been fired."
"Yes, and a fired actor can work again but a dead one can't!"

"Yes, Mel, but no director will ever hire an actor who ignores stage directions."

"Not even if the actor is drop dead handsome?"

"Not even if he acts better than Brando."

"Boy, being an actor sure is tougher than people think."

"You can say that again."

"Will I get paid to?"

"No, Mel."

"Then I'm not saying it again."

"Then this conversation is over!"

"You serious, Mel?"

Mel: "   ".

Here now is a short "Reallie" Mel and I had while watching a televised Dodger game. This "Reallie" was, for the most part, shouted:

"Swing!" Mel yelled. "That was right over the plate. Kemp, what the hell are you waiting for?"

"He was waiting on a fast ball, Mel, and the pitcher threw him a change up..."

"Which is twice as easy to hit and he struck out! Who's up?"

"Ramirez."

"Hey Ramirez," Mel shouted, "you don't win games watching soft strikes go by. Swing! Oh come on—right down the middle! You coulda hit that outta the park! You are going to lose this game for us."

"Mel, why don't you send up a pinch hitter for him?"

"I will if he doesn't swing at the next strike. Okay, that's it Ramirez! I'm sending Ethier to pinch hit for you! I'm going to get some water..."

Just as Mel stood and turned from the set, the stadium erupted as Ramirez hit one into the bleachers.

"Mel, do you think your threatening to let Ethier pinch hit helped?"

"It didn't hurt!"

A new and inspired "Reallie" was created by the team who, sixty-four years ago discovered the "Paper Cigar Band-Gold Ring Reallie". This modern "Reallie" started when Mel Brooks sat down on my living room couch and yelled "Ouch!" He had been poked by something protruding from one of my chicken-feather-filled sofa cushions. Since that memorable poke, Mel and I have been mining all six of my couch cushions for the offending feathers and we have succeeded in filling up a large freezer bag with feathers of various shapes, sizes and colors. There have been many guest pillow feather pluckers who have contributed to our bag of plucked feathers. They are Mel Brooks' lovely granddaughter Samantha Brooks, my daughter Dr. Annie Reiner, Lucas Reiner, Norman Lear, Alan Yentob (President of the BBC) and Arlene & Alan Alda.

The Original Pillow Picking Feather Pluckers

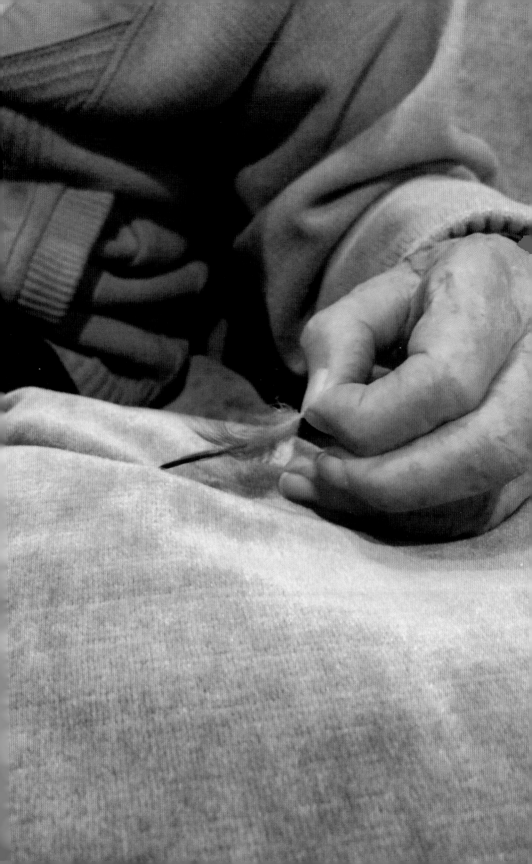

Dress Rehearsel at Rochester Summer Theater in Avon, New York, 1939

Ira Wolfer's Untimely Erection

Margrit Wyler and Carl Reiner rehearsing "Kiss The Boys Goodbye"

CHAPTER THREE

Ira Wolfer's Untimely Erection

The first year I considered myself a bonafide actor was in the summer of 1940 when I was invited to be a member of the Rochester Summer Theater. In an earlier memoir I have chronicled how I went from being an unpaid actor at the Gilmore Free Theater, to becoming a paid actor who, over two summers, received room and board for twenty-four weeks. During that time, I had the opportunity to play diverse parts, some were leading roles and some supporting ones. One role allowed me to share a stage with a revered Austrian actress, Margrit Wyler, who had fled Europe when Hitler started purging his Jewish citizens. Margrit spoke little English and had accepted the offer to work in a small summer theater so she might learn to speak our language well enough to perform some of her great classic repetoire on Broadway.

One of my more memorable roles that summer was in a play entitled "Kiss The Boys Goodbye." I don't remember much about the play but thanks to a photo I found, I do remember the snazzy suit I wore. It was an eleven dollar beauty that my mother bought for me. It was milk-white and its broad shoulders were at least an inch or two broader than mine. I do remember fondly some members of the cast, and the one that is most indelibly etched in my mind is Ellen Pruitt, a pert, five-foot-three, well-sculpted, young southern lass. She was one of three apprentice actors who paid the tuition to become members of the company.

I was much taken with Ellen, who was already 'taken' by another member of our company, a tall, blond gentile named Lawrence Slade. Larry, besides being much too handsome, had a deep voice and a slight British accent. Every morning, like clockwork, after arising and making our way from our boarding house bedrooms to the breakfast table, I would hear his resonant baritone greet me with, "Good morning, Old Shoe!"

'Old Shoe?'... I had never before been called 'Old Shoe' nor had I ever heard anyone call anyone 'Old Shoe'. At that time I would never have guessed that Larry Slade and I would become really good buddies. I think our friendship started after he saw my 'stunning performance' in "The Devil Passes." 'Stunning performance' are not my words but those used by Harriet Van Horn, the Theater Critic of The Rochester Times Union.

In the play I essayed Reverend Nicholas Lacy, a part originated on Broadway in 1932 by Basil Rathbone. At the end of one scene, while in his pulpit, Reverend Lacy rails against God. Larry, who was not in that week's production, actually said to me, "Old Shoe, it may well be that you are as good an actor as I am, or perhaps even a mite better."

Actually I did have one advantage over Larry, because he could only speak with his decidedly English accent. I was cast in all of the season's shows. I managed a credible Italian accent when playing the seventy-year-old Mr. Bonaparte in "Golden Boy" or a southern drawl as the surly cowboy, Curly, in "Of Mice and Men."

In a production of "Kiss the Boys Goodbye," both Larry and I had good roles and were supported by another buddy, Ira Wolfer, who was cast in a small part. Ira played four or five minor roles during the season. He was more of a stagehand than a thespian and had no plans to continue his acting career after the summer.

During a performance of the play, in a scene where Larry and I were downstage at the footlights having an important exchange with pretty Ellen Pruitt, Ira was seated upstage on an easy chair awaiting his cue to walk downstage and deliver a salient piece of confidential information. We gave him his cue and waited-- but no Ira and no line. The three of us glanced upstage, wondering if he had heard us. He had, and he shouted out his 'confidential line,' which was supposed to be delivered sotto voce.

Once we took our bows and the final curtain fell, we asked Ira, "Why did you deliver your line sitting in your chair?"

And here is what had happened:

During that scene, pert, pretty Ellen Pruitt, who was wearing a diaphanous silk dress and no slip, was standing in front of the footlights. Ira was paying much less attention to our dialogue than he was to the front-lit silhouetted outline of our southern belle's sexy, shapely, ever so subtly bowed legs. The scene we were enacting was long enough for him to acquire a full-blown erection, one so rigid that it ruled out any thought he had of standing up and walking downstage.

A theory has long been held that when an actor is performing before a live audience, his flow of adrenalin makes it well nigh impossible for him to get a boner. That night, in Avon, New York, on stage at the Rochester Summer Theater, Ira Wolfer put that theory to rest, or at least provided one documented exception.

Carl Reiner in "Kiss the Boys Goodbye"

Sol Pomerantz & Carl Reiner Iwo Jima 1944

The Corporal, The Con Man, and The Chupah Pole

Carl & Sol

CHAPTER FOUR

The Corporal, The Con Man and The Chupah Pole

At one point, during the Second World War, I was assigned to the Signal Corps where I was trained to be a Teletype Operator. It was at the Signal Corps School in Joplin, Missouri where I met Private Sol Pomerantz, who became my best buddy. I also met Private Herb Schwartz, who became my best buddy's worst buddy.

Herb was an egocentric who attempted to act like an altruist. He referred to himself as "The Kid" and "The Kid" was constantly offering his fellow barracks mates cookies, candies, magazines or any goodies he had cadged from the mess hall or his secret sources. Most servicemen often found themselves in a buddy relationship with a person who had similar interests, but there was no one in our platoon who had any interest in being Herb's buddy, which left him as the 'odd man out.' He was a hard man to shake and the few times we were successful in doing so, our guilt took over and we allowed him back into our circle.

Most of our days at the school were spent learning how to type at a proscribed number of words per minute and studying the procedures for the proper sending and receiving of voice and teletyped messages. After a few weeks of concentrated study, we were tested on our proficiency as typists and on our knowledge of proper Message Center procedure.

The tests were given in a large room that accommodated two platoons of trainees. First up was the typing test. The cacophonous clacking of the typewriters was a sound I had never before heard. We were all aware that if we flunked either test we would be dropped from the Signal Corps and reassigned elsewhere. The unknown, dangerous 'elsewhere' is where none of us wanted to go.

Our group included Private Fred Robbins, a quiet chap who both Sol Pomerantz and I were happy to have as a friend. Sol was, by far, the best typist, the best student, the best educated and the most even-tempered. He was just a nice guy. He was also, as Herb knew instinctively, 'a soft-touch.'

During the testing process, Herb requested "a small favor" of Sol. Herb's request, which to me, only a man with colossal 'chutzpah' (gall) could make, was for Sol to take all of his tests for him. There were two parts, one was typing skills that required us to type a certain amount of words per minute. I did fairly well but Sol aced it-his fingers were a blur on the keyboard. The other test was a written one that graded our understanding of the procedure needed to successfully run the Message Center. I was given a passing grade of eighty, and Sol managed a cool ninety-six. Herb failed both tests miserably, which meant that he would be transferred out. For some perverse reason, the Army allowed those who failed to re-take the tests. Herb knew that if he took the tests again he would fail again, but he also knew that those who monitored the tests did not know any of us. Armed with this knowledge, he dared ask Sol to take the tests for him. Sol, of course declined, saying that it was a type of crime for which, if caught, he could be faced with a court martial. Herb countered, and I was there to hear this exchange:

"Sol Buddy, if I fail again, and I know I will, they'll send me to the Infantry--into combat. I could be killed! Do you want to live your life knowing that if you had done me this one small favor, I might be alive?... Sol, I know you... you wouldn't want my blood on your hands, would you?"

Cpl. Reiner   Sgt. Schwartz   Cpl. Pomerantz

For both tests, Sol wrote Herb Schwartz's name atop the test papers and forged Herb's signature. On the written test, because Sol already knew the questions and had learned the answers to the ones he had missed, the faux Herb Schwartz scored ninety-eight, two points higher than Sol Pomerantz.

One year later, Sol's good deed had unexpected consequences.

Our group, after being certified as Signal Corps Message Center operators, was shipped to Seattle where we boarded a ship and sailed on a decidedly non-pacific, Pacific Ocean-a roiling sea that did not allow me to keep a single meal down during our long, long, long crossing on a Liberty Ship, a jerry built vessel that was not equipped with stabilizers.

After docking in Oahu, and eating my first meal in days, I learned that our group was assigned to Detachment 18, which, on the following Saturday, was scheduled to be shipped to an unknown destination. At this point, fate stepped in and changed the trajectory of my Army career and of my life. Fate had me notice a poster that hung in our Recreation Room.

It invited service men to attend a performance of Hamlet that was being held in Farrington Hall at the University Of Hawaii. It was billed as the "G. I. Hamlet" and was being performed by the Army Entertainment Section. Sol and I decided to spend our last night in Oahu soaking up culture. We were pretty sure that it was worth attending as it boasted the appearance of Maurice Evans as Hamlet. Maurice Evans had been a star on both the British and American stages and was presently, I learned, a Major in the U. S. Army. Sol and I were more than happy with what we saw that night.

Major Maurice Evans as Hamlet

Major Evans and the cast were excellent, but the happy surprise for me was the presence of the actor playing the part of Laertes. It was my old compatriot, Howard Morris. We had worked together at the NYA Radio Workshop in New York. It was a WPA project housed in the building where the "Ed Sullivan Show" later emanated and where David Letterman now holds forth.

I went backstage to congratulate Howie on his performance but before I could get a word out, he asked me if I had a comedy act.

Howie, besides acting as Laertes, was also the acting sergeant of an entertainment section administered by Major Evans. My old buddy was in charge of recruiting talent for the variety shows they sent out to entertain the troops at our Army bases.

I told Howie that I did have an act and he asked if I would audition for Major Evans and his assistant, Captain Allen Ludden. Yes, that Allen Ludden, who, after the war, hosted TV's popular game show, "Password" and married Betty White.

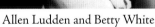
Allen Ludden and Betty White

Howard Morris

I explained to Howie that I would have like to audition but I was shipping out the following night. Sol Pomerantz suggested that even if I could not join their entertainment company, I should audition. "Find out how good you are," he counseled, "see what professionals think of your act."

The following morning, I auditioned. I did my fairly good impressions of Jimmy Stewart, Charles Boyer and Akim Tamiroff and also dared to do a Shakespearean double talk impression of Major Evans' saliva-spraying delivery, which, thankfully, did not seem to upset him.

Both he and his aide, Captain Ludden, agreed that I would be a welcome addition to their troupe and, with the aid of General Richardson, the head of the Central Pacific Base Command, I was transferred to Major Evans' entertainment section and performed at Army bases throughout the Central Pacific.

A year later, the war with Germany and Japan came to an end, and miraculously I found myself on Iwo Jima at a base camp, entertaining my old outfit, which included my buddies Sol Pomerantz, Fred Robbins and their nemesis, Herb Schwartz. Sol was so happy, not only to see us but also to tell us that a court martial he had been facing had just been called off. He quietly told me of the Damocles sword that had been hanging over his head for weeks.

He took a deep breath and related how, as Corporal in charge of the message center, he had sent and received all voice and teletype messages that flowed in and out of the Command Post. He told of a voice message he had received three days before the Japanese officially surrendered, informing him that the "war was over."

At that time, no one knew that the voice came from a lonely G.I. who, while strolling along a beach in San Francisco, decided to play war correspondent and excitedly announced over his mobile walkie-talkie, "The war is over! Japan surrendered!" These words were picked up by a nearby Message Center and rebroadcast all over the Pacific. Sol heard that announcement, and even though he knew the end of the war was imminent, he followed procedure and asked the sender to identify himself and authenticate his message by using the proscribed language, which he did not do. Sol guessed there was something fishy about the announcement and refused to pass it on. Sol's best judgement, however, was over ruled and, after a long, heated argument, Corporal Pomerantz reluctantly obeyed the command of his screaming, red-faced superior, Staff Sargeant Herb Schwartz!

I could not believe that "The Kid," the insufferable Herb Schwartz, had become Sol Pomerantz's superior officer, and when I asked Sol how in the world such a preposterous thing could happen, Sol shrugged and said, "Herb had better credentials."

I knew immediately that Sol was referring to the test scores. When the officer in charge checked the two candidates' scores, he learned that both Private Pomerantz and Private Schwartz were excellent typists, but in the written tests on authentication procedures, Private Pomerantz scored a 96 and Private Schwartz, a 98. Herb, who took neither test and never learned one thing about the whole operation, was now Sol's boss. For almost a year Sol had been running a model operation but received no credit for it. Had Sol admitted that he had taken the test for Herb, Sol would have faced a court-martial.

The unauthenticated voice message announcing the war's end, that Herb ordered Sol to relay, was picked up by operators in places as far away as the Philippine Islands. It was there, at an ammunition storage facility that some exuberant G. I.s' celebrated the great news by exploding one of the bombs they were guarding. The explosion detonated other bombs that demolished the Quonset hut and killed some of the personnel in it.

For having passed on the illegal message that had fatal consequences, both Cpl. Pomerantz and his superior, Staff Sgt. Schwartz faced major disciplinary action. What saved their asses and caused a dismissal of their pending arraignment was the fact that a commissioned officer was not present in the Message Center when the illegal voice message was relayed. At that crucial time, the on-duty Captain was in the Rec Hall sipping a cold beer with a fellow officer. The Captain, for ignoring proscribed Army procedure, now awaited trial.

It took the end of two wars, one in Europe and one in the Pacific, for Sol to reclaim a life that did not include "The Kid."

Sol and I were mustered out of the service about the same time and managed to stay in touch. We both lived in New York, my wife, Estelle and I in the Bronx, Sol and his fiancée, Naomi, on Long Island. Herb Schwartz was also a New Yorker, and both Sol and I worked hard to keep "The Kid" from knowing our whereabouts. When Sol and Naomi decided to marry, they invited a number of old Army buddies to their wedding. Sol made a point of telling us he worried that "The Kid" would find out about the ceremony and show up. Sol asked that we not discuss his impending marriage with anyone—especially where it was to be held, which was on the back lawn of his bride-to-be's Long Island home.

Two or three days before the wedding, Sol called me to ask if there had been any Herb sightings and I was happy to report that "The Kid" had not contacted any of us and, as far as I knew, he was not aware of the wedding.

The day of the wedding, Sol chose four of us, each to hold one of the canopy poles that supported the 'Chuppah,' under which, the bride, the groom, the best man and the Rabbi would be standing. The four consisted of Sol's three Army buddies, Fred Robbins, Frank Gagliardi, me and a cousin of Sol's.

It was a perfect day for an outdoor wedding; the sky was blue, the sun shone brightly and a soft breeze blew as Sol's lovely bride strode down the aisle and joined her smiling groom under the Chuppah. The Rabbi nodded to the happy couple, opened his Bible and just as he began to speak, his attention shifted to something going on at the house. What was going on was the hurried entrance of a well-dressed man making his way to the Chuppah.

"Sol, The Kid is here!" Herb shouted. "Sorry I'm late!"

With that ,"The Kid" grabbed the pole Sol's cousin was holding and said, "I'll take it from here!"

"The Kid" then ordered the Rabbi to continue the ceremony, which the confused man did. All present had the same thought, "It's more important that Sol and Naomi get married than "The Kid" gets punched in the nose!"

At the luncheon, "The Kid" continued to operate, going from table to table and introducing himself as Sol's former commanding officer on Iwo Jima.

When it came to toasting the newlyweds, "The Kid" was the first one to jump up and offer his heartfelt congratulations to "The best soldier any commanding officer ever had!"

Sol smiled, looked toward me and shrugged. "The Kid" did all he could to ruin Sol's wedding but thankfully, he couldn't.

Blessedly, soon after Sol's wedding, "The Kid" disappeared from our lives. Paradoxically, it was because "The Kid" had crashed Sol's wedding that he caught a real break. It was there "The Kid" met a corrugated box manufacturer who was looking for a live wire to energize his firm's sales department. "The Kid" jumped at the opportunity and moved to Florida from where, periodically, Sol and I would get a progress report. He boasted about how well he was doing managing a plant that employed more than a hundred workers. He raptured how much he loved living in sunny Florida, his newly adopted state. I recall his writing about someone with whom he had become romantically involved. Later on, I also remember getting cards from him saying that he had enjoyed seeing me perform on TV. "The Kid" had definitely mellowed. It appeared that the love of a good woman had turned "The Kid" into someone who could pass for an adult. Note: I had no idea that twenty years after my days in the Army, I would create the Dick Van Dyke Show and write an episode that featured Dick as Rob Petrie being visited by his old Army buddy. At first I thought of protecting Sol Pomerantz's privacy by giving the character a fictitious name, but then I thought that rather than protecting his privacy, it might delight him and his wife and kids if they heard his name telecast nationwide. And it did.

Dick Van Dyke as Rob Petrie, Allan Melvin as Sol Pomerantz

USO Dance Volunteers

Teaching Joyce Kuntz to Pronounce Her Name Correctly

CHAPTER FIVE

Teaching Joyce Kuntz to Pronounce Her Name Correctly

Way back in 1943, when all the world's civilized nations banded together to defeat the scourge that was Adolf Hitler, I was a Private First Class in the United States Army and stationed in Washington D.C. I have written of this time in my bio, "I Remember Me," but for those who, for some reason, missed the opportunity to read it, let me set the scene. A number of us G. I.s were billeted at Georgetown University where we were enrolled as students in their School of Foreign Service. After ten months of extensive training, my buddies and I were awarded diplomas that designated us as French language interpreters.

It was during that stay at Georgetown where Sol Pomerantz and I became best buddies. We often spent part of our twenty-four hour passes at the local USO ballroom in downtown Washington D.C. One Sunday afternoon as we ventured into the sparsely inhabited ballroom, Sol left to find some beer. No sooner had he left, than I turned and saw a blonde-haired vision approaching me. She was wearing an expensive looking waist-hugging dress and was flashing the broadest, whitest, most perfect teeth in the history of smiles. Her first words were delivered with the deepest southern drawl I had ever heard. They were:

"Hiiyuh, Cahwpurull, wailcum tuh thuh Yeww Ayyss Ohw!"

Being a fledgling interpreter, I quickly translated her words to mean, "Hi Corporal, welcome to the USO!"

I said, "Hi," and when she asked my name, I said that it was Carl Reiner. She then gracefully extended her bare, lovely milk-white arm and offered me her lace-gloved hand. As we shook hands she introduced herself by announcing loudly, "Ah yam Joyce Cunts!"

For a moment I did not believe I had heard right and asked her to repeat her name. When she did, and I realized that I had heard it correctly the first time, I asked softly,

"Your name is Joyce Cunts?"

"Yes," she shot back, giggling, "Joyce Jessica Cunts."

I thought: *Was she putting me on? Did she see in me a gullible New Yorker with whom she decided to have some fun?*

I looked into her big, clear blue trusting eyes and decided that she was not putting me on. I thought: *Where did she come from? Did she not know her name's common usage? Had no one in her family, no one of her friends, no one in her community ever heard the most universally accepted vulgar term for a woman's private part?*

From the sweet, quizzical expression on her face, and her excitedly telling me that this was her first time away from her small town, somewhere outside of Opelika, Georgia. It was literally her first day away from home and I knew that she had absolutely no idea what I was thinking and what I was about to tell her... for her own good. Attempting to be a kind Dutch uncle, I asked her how she spelled her last name and she said, "K U N T Z zactly haow it souwands," then repeated its pronunciation, "Cunts!"

Hesitantly, I informed her that my last name, Reiner, was of German origin as was her name, and that K u n t z, in Germany would be pronounced, "Koontz".

"Koooontz," she giggled, then said, "now thayats sooo silly!"

"It may seem so," I told her, "but if you keep pronouncing your name in a non-Germanic way it gives it a meaning that most people..."

"Whut," she asked naively. "Whut'll mos folk thyink I meah if'n ah say mah nayam is Cunts?"

I told her as gently as I could, that her name or the way she pronounced it, was a slang word for vagina.

Joyce glared at me and before I could say another word Sol Pomerantz returned. Joyce Kuntz wheeled angrily and, to prove how off base I was, she extended her white-gloved hand to Sol and announced defiantly, "May nayim is Cunts, Joyce Cunts! Whut's yours?"

"Sol Pomerantz," he shot back, "Nice to meet you Joyce Cunts!"

Sol then burst out laughing, punched me on the arm and congratulated Joyce on being a good sport by going along with, what he thought was a sick joke.

After Sol learned the truth, he and I spent a good deal of time convincing Joyce that, while she was away from her home and hearth, she use the Germanic pronunciation of her name, "Koontz." And that is my story. Oh, I do admit that I may have embellished some of the dialogue, but I've changed none of the names. It may be hard for skeptics to believe, but this 70-year-old tale I just told, is true!

I Pagliacci
Vesti La Giubba
R. Leoncavalo

Enrico Caruso

Giovanni Martinelli

Jan Peerce

Three Operatic Tenors, Two I Owe and One Owes Me

ENRICO CARU
COPYRIGHT
BY LAVECCHA.ST
CHICAGO
NO. 3.

CHAPTER SIX

Three Operatic Tenors, Two I Owe and One Owes Me

Very early on, when I was thirteen, I became enamored of a tenor voice that I heard bellowing from the horn of the Gramophone that sat on our dining room table. The Gramophone, or Victrola was a boxy device that my father used to play his RCA Red Seal recordings. Captured in the grooves of these black acetate records, were the voices of the great operatic singers, the performances of virtuoso instrumentalists and the world's great Philharmonic symphony orchestras of the era.

This particular recording that my father played for me featured an aria from the opera "Pagliacci." It was sung by a tenor whose name I learned was Enrico Caruso. I had no idea what he was singing about or why I was starting to get goose bumps.

Yesterday, at my computer, after I Googled: (*Operatic tenor, Enrico Caruso*), I was rewarded with the date of his birth, Feb. 25, 1873, and of his passing, Aug. 2, 1921. Along with these statistics, I heard the voice of Caruso singing "Vesti La Giubba," and the goose bumps I experienced as a thirteen year old were nowhere near the size or intensity of the goose bumps I was now feeling.

Throughout the years I had made it a point to hear all of the great tenors' recordings of that signature aria from Leoncavallo's opera "Pagliacci." Included in that vaunted group were Italy's Beniamino Gigli, considered to be Caruso's closest rival, Ferruccio Tagliavini, Tito Schipa, Richard Tauber, Jussi Bjorling, Richard Crooks, Jan Peerce, Nino Martini, Mario Lanza, Frederick Jagel, and Giovanni Martinelli.

Which brings me to the one operatic performer to whom I am beholden, Giovanni Martinelli.

Giovanni Martinelli

In 1939, when I was seventeen, I was privileged to attend Signor Martinelli's solo concert at New York's Town Hall. At that event I saw and heard the great tenor do something that I have appropriated and have used with great success in my role as the Host or Emcee of many of our industry's award shows.

During the concert, I looked forward to hearing the great tenor render his version of "E Lucevan le Stelle" from Puccini's "La Tosca." He was in great voice and the crowd responded appropriately. He had just sung the opening recitative and was approaching the high note in that first phrase when the maestro's voice cracked. It was a vocal clinker of the first magnitude and audible gasps escaped from everyone in the audience. It was then, that Giovanni Martinelli did the most unexpected thing–he looked about as if he were trying to hear something... and then he started to laugh, not softly but hysterically– and he continued to laugh so long and hard, while wiping tears from his eyes. It was at this point, while still laughing that he shouted, "DID YOU HEAR DAT!? DID YOU HEAR DAT!? HAH?" The audience laughed and shouted, "Yes!" which spurred him on.

"What do you say…" he chortled, "should…we try again?"

The audience laughed and applauded as a grinning Martinelli looked into the orchestra pit, waved to the conductor and shouted, "Maestro, we try again! From the top!"

The conductor nodded, cued the orchestra; Giovanni Martinelli took a deep breath and started to sing. This time that high note came soaring out of him and it was a heavenly sound. The audience greeted it with a burst of applause that only true opera aficionados would know to deliver. Ordinarily, a singer receives this kind of reception after he hits the last high note at the end of his aria, never at the very beginning of it.

Martinelli, without breaking stride, acknowledged the audience's approval with a wink. He then went on to give us a brilliant rendition of Puccini's "E Lucevan le Stelle." The applause he received for this particular aria was the loudest and most sustained of the evening.

I was reminded of a trapeze artist I once saw at the Ringling Brothers' Circus. While flying through the air from one trapeze to another, he missed catching one and fell some hundred feet into the net below. He naturally made a successful second attempt which garnered him much applause and a standing ovation.

I am beholden to Signor Martinelli because that night at Town Hall I learned something from him that has made my hosting award dinners a tad more entertaining. My mantra, had that word existed then, would have been: "Go with the flow!" If, as our tenor did, you hit a clinker attempting to hit a high note, don't try to hide it-- acknowledge it and use it! One time, I had fun when trying to read a teleprompter that was scrolling too fast. I read the copy at breakneck speed and when I stopped to take a breath, I instructed the operator to slow the machine down, which he did, but this time it ran too slow, and I exaggerated its speed by reading and gesticulating in slow motion.

I was once confronted with the task of introducing four or five starlets whom I had seen backstage but never before met. I read off their names from a list I had been handed and I asked them to join me at the podium. I had the wrong list but confidently announced five men's names. It was not hard to get big laughs when calling exquisitely gowned, gorgeous women Herman Mankiewicz, Robert Aldrich, Victor Fleming, Alfred Hitchcock and Norman Jewison. I don't remember the actual names I announced fifty years ago but they were of this ilk.

One other memorable gaff, I have already covered in an earlier book but it illustrates my premise. As the Emcee of a Young Musicians' benefit, I tripped over a small amplifier on my way to the podium. I fell hard enough to tear the ligament in my left kneecap and rip my quadriceps off the bone in my right leg.

"Is there a Doctor in the house?" I shouted a moment after landing.

That line produced the biggest laugh of the night. Too many in the audience thought I had done the pratfall as a gag.

While lying onstage at the Beverly Hilton Hotel and in need of medical attention, I followed "Is there a doctor in the house?" with, "Is there a comedian in the house?" which got me another big laugh. It also got me my old friend, Louis Nye who was in the audience. As I lay there waiting for the ambulance, Louis went on to 'do his act' and completely ignored my presence. The memory of the pain I felt that night is gone but the memory of the laughter lingers.

So far I have described the reasons I am beholden to Caruso and Martinelli. I owe Enrico Caruso for exciting me about the tenor voice and the operatic singers who use it, and I owe Giovanni Martinelli for informing my abilities as an M.C. The only one of the trio of tenors who owes me a debt is Jan Peerce.

In 1938, when I was sixteen, Jan Peerce was on the cusp of becoming one of the most celebrated tenors of his time and I would feel partly responsible for his achieving that fame, having done something to make key people aware of his great talent.

I first heard Mr. Peerce sing on radio as a guest of the great Arturo Toscanini, who conducted the NBC Symphony Orchestra. The short, unprepossessing tenor was one of the Maestro's favorite artists, and because my father never missed a Sunday afternoon concert, I heard Peerce's great tenor voice dozens of times. Whenever Jan Peerce appeared at Radio City Music Hall, I was there.

Every Saturday afternoon, when my father tuned in to hear the Metropolitan Opera House broadcast, I waited to hear the tenors sing their arias and I would compare their vocal talents to that of my favorite, Jan Peerce. My father did not disagree with my assessment, so armed with the consensus in my home and the passion of a sixteen-year-old fanatic tenor lover; I dashed off a letter to the Manager of the Met, a Mr. Giulio Gotti-Casazza:

Jan Peerce

47

March 10, 1938

> *Dear Mr. Gotti-Casazza,*
>
> *I listen to your opera broadcasts every Saturday and I enjoy them very much. You have many wonderful tenors singing at the Met and I think that Jan Peerce is someone you should consider hiring as he has a thrilling voice. Arturo Toscanini has often praised both his voice and musicianship.*
> *I hope you will consider making Jan Peerce a member of the Metropolitan Opera Company.*
>
> *Gratefully,*
> *Carl Reiner*

P.S. Mr. Peerce has many, many fans who feel as I do.

I did not receive an answer from Mr. Gotti-Casazza but I was happy I had sent it.

I just surprised myself by remembering the name Gotti-Casazza. I have never heard his name uttered or seen it in print and to be sure I was not remembering something I made up, I Googled his name and lo and behold, I did not make it up.

In 1939 when I was seventeen years old and still a devoted fan of Jan Peerce, I bought two tickets to Mr. Peerce's first full recital at New York's Town Hall. Accompanying me was my girlfriend and fellow actor, Barbara Komack. We had met in an acting class and found, besides liking each other, we both liked opera. Having a very low paying job as a delivery boy, I could only afford the cheapest seats, which were in the balcony.

The seventeen scheduled songs that were listed in the program, I knew well, and Mr. Peerce, who was in excellent voice, did justice to them all. After each selection he was rewarded by thunderous applause. I was almost ecstatic; I say almost because missing from the scheduled seventeen arias was my particular favorite, "Rachel, quand du seigneur..." an aria from Halevy's opera "La Juive." I had bought a Victor recording of it and had played it at home many, many times. At the end of the concert, more encores are expected and he delivered.

He obliged with a rollicking rendition of "Mattinata," a virtuoso, triple tonguing favorite. As he accepted the deserved applause, I stood up and shouted as loudly as I could, "LA JUIVE, LA JUIVE, LA JUIVE!" He looked up at me, waved his hand in my direction, nodded to his accompanist and delivered a thrilling rendition of this soaring aria. I have never before shouted out a request, and was thunderstruck that Mr. Peerce actually heard me and accommodated me. His passionate interpretation of the aria was greeted with wild applause.

He had dashed off the stage and when he returned, he had a coat draped over his arm and, before he could address the audience, I stood up again and shouted a request for another Caruso favorite from Georges Bizet's "Pearl Fishers".

I shouted, "PEARL FISHERS, PEARL FISHERS!"

Peerce held up his hand, looked in my direction. "I am sorry," he apologized, "I would love to sing that aria but I just received word that my wife is on her way to the hospital... our first baby is due--I'm sure you understand... so if you'll excuse me..."

With that, Jan Peerce dashed off the stage, the applause and the shouted good wishes following him into the wings and out the stage door.

Some forty years later, I was hosting a televised industry awards show and the director in charge was a chap named Larry Peerce. When he introduced himself to me, I said, "Hey, I was at Town Hall the night your father refused to sing an encore because he said your mother..."

"...was on her way to the hospital to deliver me" he interrupted. "He loved telling that story."

In 1941, when I was 19 years old, Jan Peerce made an auspicious debut at the Metropolitan playing the role of Alfredo in Verdi's "La Traviata." I am not saying that my letter to Gotti Casazza was the reason he hired Jan Peerce, but I am also not **NOT** saying it was not the reason. What I am certain of is that I must really feel that way. Why else would I have spent this last paragraph bringing it to the world's attention?

Fidel Castro, Cuba 1960

Jack Paar Tells Tales of Castro, Cuba and Castration

General Fulgencio Batista

CHAPTER SEVEN

Jack Paar Tells Tales of Castro, Cuba and Castration

It was 1960, and after a lovely dinner at Dinah Shore's home, Jack Paar told me a mesmerizing story.

Jack had flown out from New York to appear on a most popular musical-variety show, aptly called, "The Dinah Shore Show." It was a show on which, along with Charles Isaacs, I was a writer and also a performer. Each week we had guest stars such as Frank Sinatra and Yves Montand, and they were billed as a "Special Guest Star!" I performed every other week and was billed as a "Not So Special Guest Star." After the show, on which Jack Paar was the special guest, Dinah invited Jack, my wife Estelle and me to her home for one of her personally cooked gourmet dinners. Jack, who was not a calm man, was particularly jumpy that night. He had just returned from Cuba, where he had personally arranged a one-on-one interview with Fidel Castro, the triumphant leader of the revolution against the Fascistic dictator, General Fulgencio Batista. Jack Paar had managed to scoop every seasoned newsperson in the world. After dinner, Jack quietly asked me to join him for a private chat about his trip to Cuba. He made a point of not wanting to share his story with Dinah or my wife. I will never forget what he told me that night or the quiver in his voice when he described the details of a most unnerving event.

"I never dreamed," Jack began, speaking softly, "that Fidel Castro would accept my offer to interview him but for some reason he trusted that, because I was a talk show host and not a hard nosed journalist, I might report his story as he wanted it reported."

I remember thinking, as the whole country was, 'A late night TV comedian scoops the likes of Walter Cronkite, Mike Wallace, Edward R. Murrow and the major anchormen of every national and international news organization in the world! It's nuts!'

Jack told me of arriving in Havana early in the evening and being met by a driver who escorted him to the Havana Hilton Hotel, where Castro then resided. The driver's only words to Jack before he took off were "Wait here, someone will take you up to Senor Castro!"

Jack said that it was close to midnight when he sat down, and had to wait for three hours before a non-uniformed vassal came to escort him to a second floor bedroom where Fidel and one of his Lieutenants were making plans for the following day—plans that would include Jack's participation. Jack said that he was amazed that there were no armed guards about to protect, The Chief, or "El Jefe," as he was called. The country had gone through a revolution and Jack had expected to see lots of soldiers bustling about, but all was strangely quiet--everything seemed to be under control.

Jack said that he was ushered into a bedroom and told that Castro would meet with him early in the morning. He got very little sleep that night and could not believe that he was going to speak with the man who every newsman in the world would give an eyetooth to interview.

Early the next morning, after eating the small breakfast offered him, Jack said he was visited by Fidel, who shook his hand and bade him welcome. Castro informed Jack, as he escorted him to a waiting car, that they were going to visit some of the mansions that General Fulgencio Batista had called home. Castro showed Jack but two of the half dozen palatial estates Batista had either built or appropriated during his bloody reign. Jack became more and more excited as he described the mansions with their plush velvet draped windows, tapestried walls and works of art that were set in gold-leafed frames. In each home, hanging in every ornate living room were full length, oil portraits of Batista, wearing a colorful, be-medaled army uniform.

"And in every one of his palatial homes," Jack reported, "in every plushy bedroom were clothes closets, the length of a single freight car, and when Fidel opened the sliding doors I saw what must have been fifty uniforms—and all exactly like the one in that oil portrait of Batista. Well, not exactly." he corrected. "They all had the same chest-full of medals, gold braid and epaulets but they were of different colors—red, black, purple, white, khaki, grey, you name it, he had it."

We both agreed that Batista, besides being ruthless, was a nut cake, but Jack insisted that what Castro showed him later that day was something that he was afraid would haunt his dreams forever.

"I don't think I'll ever get a full night's sleep again!" is the way Jack put it.

Jack then went on to describe unimaginable scenes of horror that I have never forgotten and frankly was not sure I wanted to include in this book.

Jack mentioned the names of two locales he visited, Oriente Province and Pinar Del Rey. He went there ostensibly to meet some of the citizens who had helped Castro to liberate Cuba. I specifically recall the names because the Panatela cigars I smoked at that time bore those two names, Oriente and Pinar del Rey.

On the ride to Oriente Province, Jack had asked Castro how he had gone about starting a revolution and he said, "I did not start a revolution! No one person can start a revolution. I joined a revolution that started when many of our people could no longer abide the miserable living conditions that General Batista had forced upon us. We all had no choice but to look for a way out. Batista and the land owners controlled all the tobacco, cotton, banana and pineapple plantations and they hired our people to cultivate, plant and harvest all of their crops-- for which they received the equivalent of one dollar a week-yes, a week, not a dollar an hour or even a dollar a day!"

Paar, then, stuttering more than usual, described the trips he took to the two of Cuba's Provinces.

"When we arrived at Oriente," Jack related, "we were greeted warmly by a throng of townsfolk and after acknowledging them, Castro asked the women to return to their homes and the men to gather in the square." He proceeded to explain that the men who stood there were farmers who earned a dollar a week for their efforts.

They had never joined a union or even known that unions existed until they were invited to hear a representative of the farm worker's union explain how their lives would be better if they were members of a union. Paar made a point of saying that these men did nothing more than listen to a man talk about a union.

Then Jack said, "Castro shouted something in Spanish, that I never ever expected but understood. He yelled, "Would all of you please pull down your pants. I wish for my American friend to see what Batista has done to you."

While approximately two hundred men reluctantly and embarrassedly started to drop their trousers, Castro explained that when Batista had learned that these peasants met with a union leader, he ordered that, as punishment, they all be castrated!

"I could not believe my eyes," Jack Paar said, "and I looked away, but Castro said, 'Do not look away... you must see what this monster has done so you can tell the world about it!'"

As Jack described what he saw, his stuttering became more and more pronounced. He said that Castro insisted that he look "first hand" so he could go on American television and give an eye witness account of the barbaric procedures General Batista's surgeons had performed on his people.

For the next few minutes, Jack described something I had difficulty picturing. He spoke of being on the verge of fainting in the town square, and looking away as he walked among the hundreds of bare-assed men.

"Senor Paar," Castro pleaded, "Do not look away. I beg you, however distasteful or grotesque it is, you must look directly at these men's mutilated groins. If you see clearly what Batista has done to these men, you will be able to speak clearly of it! By reporting these horrors, you can help to bring justice to our citizens in Oriente Province and our homeland."

"I told Castro that I would. I could never imagine anything more horrible, but that was before he drove us to Pinar del Rey. Here, instead of two hundred peasants being castrated, General Batista had chopped the balls off of five hundred of his fellow citizens. Fidel felt that I had to see that too—and damn it, I saw it!"

This meeting and conversation, as I said, took place in 1960, exactly fifty-three years ago. The incidents that Jack Paar described were exactly as I remembered them. I actually googled, Castro, Paar and the Cuban revolution and found that my long-term memory is still something I can trust. On Wikipedia, I learned: *Many of Batista's soldiers, appalled at using castration and torture that they were ordered to carry out upon innocent civilians, defected to Castro's rebels.*

Jack Paar host of The Tonight Show. (1957-1962)

In 1983 Jack Paar wrote an autobiography, "P.S. Jack Paar," published by Doubleday. From what I understand the tale that Jack Paar told me at Dinah's house was originally included in that book, but for whatever reason, it was edited from the final draft.

HOLLYWOOD FOREIGN PRESS ASSOCIATION

The Once Tarnished Golden Globes

Mary Tyler Moore, Dick VanDyke & Carl Reiner on the set

CHAPTER EIGHT

The Once Tarnished Golden Globes

Today the motion picture industry considers the "Golden Globes" to be one of Hollywood's most important and influential organizations. A film that wins a "Golden Globe" for Best Picture is thought to be in line for at least an Oscar nomination.

In 1964 the organization was considered to be neither influential nor important, and winning a Golden Globe was not something about which any filmmaker or actor would boast. The resumes and reputations of its members was an industry joke. A few dozen people, who called themselves journalists, formed the organization in 1943. They wrote for small European trade publications that advertised the goods sold in the local stores. These free 'publications,' commonly called 'throw-aways,' were sometimes no more than a single sheet.

In that same year, 1964, while writing and producing "The Dick Van Dyke Show," my secretary informed me that our show was nominated for a Golden Globe award. Knowing the reputation of the voting members as being inept news reporters and 'ept' freeloaders, I was not thrilled with the honor. "Freeloaders" was the description hung on them by legitimate reviewers who claimed that these gentlemen were only in the business to get invites to studio shindigs so they could cadge free food and drinks. Most of the film studios publicity departments felt that being able to send out an announcement that one of their films received an award, whatever the auspices, was twice as good as not being able to send out an announcement.

As the producer of "The Dick Van Dyke Show," I was informed that our show was nominated for a Golden Globe and I was invited to attend their event. I was made aware of the time, date and venue for the award ceremony and I thanked them for the show's nomination but informed them that I was busy and unable to attend.

In previous years, I had seen their televised awards shows and, like most viewers, found them to be perversely entertaining. I also felt pain for the nominated artists who, for whatever reason, had chosen to attend the event.

On the day of the "Golden Globes" telecast, I received two or three phone calls begging me to attend and I very politely declined, telling them I was busy rehearsing "The Dick Van Dyke Show." It was the last phone call I received from someone at the "Golden Globes" that somehow convinced me that it was important for me to be at The Palladium at such and such a time.

"You must be there!" he insisted. "You will not be sorry!"

Without telling me how he knew, he made me understand that if I came to the event, I would walk out with a Golden Globe. He said he knew of someone who had foreknowledge of the results.

After chatting it over with Dick Van Dyke, we decided that I should go. I had just time to run home, toss on a tux and get to the Palladium. I was glad I did, for many reasons, not the least being that it has given me this opportunity to retell this small almost embarrassing tale. After an acceptable dinner, the dual Masters of Ceremonies, Swedish twin brothers, Gustav and Bertil Unger, each wearing a monocle in his left eye, stepped to the dias and announced that the award ceremony would begin.

One by one, they read off a list of nominations for the best acted, written and directed shows in films and television, and each and every time a winner was announced, some tuxedoed person would stride to the stage and say something like: "I am obviously not (name of winner) but he asked me to convey to you how sorry he is that, due to a prior commitment (or illness), he could not be here tonight, but wanted you to know how proud he is to receive this award."

After five or six of these awards were picked up by proxies, I started to worry that I would look like a 'schmuck' if I was the only one who picked up my own award. Members of the audience began to chuckle discreetly each time the winner was not present. The chuckles stopped when it was announced that Mickey Rooney was the winner of an acting award and in the rear of the room, someone shouted out, "There he is, he's on his way!" All eyes were on 'Mickey' as he made his way along the extreme left aisle. I remember wondering why one of the biggest stars in Hollywood was given such a bad seat. The spotlight followed the five-foot two-inch actor, and the applause grew as he reached the first row, but it stopped when 'Mickey' did not make his way to the stage, but took a left turn and entered a door marked "Men's Room". The audience did not chuckle but exploded in laughter when they realized that the short person was not Mickey Rooney. The Unger brothers explained that Mickey was indisposed and that they would accept the award for him. You will have to believe me, but every award that night was accepted by someone other than the actual winner. I believe, but I am not certain, that I was the last award or one of the last. Perhaps I remember it as the last award, as I hastened to leave as soon as I received it. Here now, is what happened when I heard one of the Swedish, monocled twins call my name. I made my way up onto the stage and as I walked toward the podium, I thought of how I would handle being the sole winner who would be picking up his own Golden Globe. The following is pretty close to what I said that night:

"I am so terribly embarrassed and I apologize for coming onstage to accept this wonderful honor. I was not intending to be here tonight. I had plans to go out to dinner with my wife and some friends and I asked my good friend Marlon Brando if he would pick up my award for me and he said that he would be happy to. He was all dressed to go but at the last minute something came up and he called me in a panic. He told me that he could not pick up the award and asked, as a personal favor, if I could pick it up myself. So, once again I must apologize—instead of seeing the great Marlon Brando picking up my Globe, you see me doing it. Sorry!"

I walked off to enough laughter to make me feel 'I done good.'

Get Behind That Big Wooden Crate
And Don't Move!

CHAPTER NINE

Get Behind That Big Wooden Crate And Don't Move!

About a year ago I was approached by a producer who invited me to be a part of a project that sounded rather interesting. It would require me to be photographed for a book of portraits that included fifty well known people, which, he informed me, would include the likes of Robert DeNiro, Jay Leno, Tracey Ullman, William Shatner, Ringo Starr, Jack Black, Amy Poehler, Seth Rogen, Snoop Dogg, Russell Brand, Archbishop Desmond Tutu and Sarah Silverman. How could I say no? I couldn't and didn't.

Not too long after, 'this producer' published a rather handsome ten by eight, hard cover, coffee table book, in which I am proud to say, I am neither seen nor mentioned.

Here now is how I got myself edited out of 'this producer's' masterwork.

One cool, cloudy day, 'this producer' had arranged for a car and driver to pick me up and take me to a building somewhere in Los Angeles. I cannot remember where this building is located. I do remember that for the occasion, I chose to wear a blue blazer, tan slacks and a fairly colorful tie. It was the tie I had permanently borrowed from Johnny Carson when I guested on his show. On it, near the bottom is a tiny sedate monogram, J.C. To pay homage to the best ever TV host, I often wear it when I appear on television.

'This producer' had arranged for us to meet in the lobby of this office building where, accompanied by a still photographer, he escorted me to an elevator that took us to the top floor, which was the thirtieth. Not too many words of conversation were exchanged, but I was given many words of instruction pertaining to where he wanted to take the shot of me. When we left the elevator, 'this producer' opened a heavy metal door and ushered me onto the roof, where we were met by a cool mist, which I thought was rain but soon learned that the moisture was coming not from the sky but from large, noisy, mushroom shaped, air conditioners. I was not at all comfortable walking around a wet roof and I asked 'this producer' to snap my picture and get me home. He said he would as soon as I get to the location he had chosen for me. To get there, he asked me to climb a narrow, metal flight of wet stairs to a small, wooden crate that sat behind one of the giant turbines.

"You gotta be kidding!" I shouted over the whirring of the air conditioner and he shouted back that he was not kidding.

I had half a mind to pack it in but the words "the show must go on," an adage that I have heeded all my theatrical life, bid me make my way up the flight of slippery steps. By clutching onto the wet banister, I managed to overcome my fear of falling to my death and arrived at my station, shaky but ready to perform.

'This gentleman' directed me to get behind that wooden crate and to sit on a small stool that had been set there. Reluctantly, I did so, then poked my head out from around the corner of the crate and shouted,

"Okay, I'm ready! Take your picture!"

And he shouted back, "I will, as soon as you pull your head back in."

And I said, "You mean you want to shoot a picture of me without me being seen?"

"That's the concept!" he said.

And I said, "Your concept is to take a picture of a celebrity while he's hidden from view?!"

"Exactly!" he said.

And I said, "But how will the readers know that I was behind that box?"

And he said, "You'll sign a paper saying that you were!"

And I said, "Fuck You!"

I then stood up, walked to the ladder, carefully made my way down it, negotiated my way past all the air conditioning turbines, and left the roof through the heavy metal door. Keeping pace with me as I strode toward the elevators was the photographer and 'this producer,' whom I verbally assaulted with a barrage of the most salacious language I had ever used in my life. On the ride down in the elevator, a never ending flow of vile, dirty words just flew off my tongue and tumbled out of my mouth-- the volume increased as I followed him off the elevator, through the lobby, out the revolving doors and into his waiting limo. I stopped spewing scatological venom at him only after his limo had sped out of sight.

Throughout my harangue, there were many open-mouthed, gawking bystanders who must have wondered what had provoked one human being to sound off so angrily at another human being.

If I felt any guilt or compunction about maligning 'this gentleman' it all but disappeared when I looked through a copy of his book that was just recently published. I will not mention its title for fear of enhancing sales.

I feel it is noteworthy that throughout the book, that there are signed letters from unknown onlookers testifying that the unseen participant in each photo was actually there. I believe that of all the actual participants, who were not seen in the hidden celebrity photos, not one signed saying that he was there.

I am sadly aware that even though it is no longer possible for an entrepreneur to find a buyer for the Brooklyn Bridge, 'this producer' will likely find enough buyers to make him happy and to piss me off.

The Mystery Of The Gold Money Clip
and The Rubber Band

CHAPTER TEN

The Mystery Of The Gold Money Clip
and The Rubber Band

On my daily walks around the block, I have for the past few years seen many folded, 'throw-away' local newspapers lying on front lawns or in driveways. The ones on the lawns are usually wet from the lawn sprinklers. In 1961, when I first moved into my home, I would pick them up, scan them and then toss them in the trashcan. As time went on, instead of picking them up I would kick them into the gutter where they would be swept up by a city owned street sweeper. The two papers were, and still are, "The Beverly Hills Courier" and the ""Beverly Hills WEEKLY" and except for a political essay or two, they are primarily shopping guides that inform us what is on sale at the super markets and which homes are for sale. (On the cover of this week's "The Beverly Hills WEEKLY," which minutes ago I retrieved from my front lawn, is a 'brief,' announcing that Sinai Temple will conduct same sex marriages.)

The one thing that the "Courier" and the "WEEKLY" had in common was the rubber band that kept these twice folded 'throw-aways' from being scattered by a wind. After many years of my daily strolls, I concluded that most homeowners have never read them or even bothered to pick them up. No one paid attention to these orphaned freebies. They may have lain there forever had I not acted. I made it possible for Mother Nature to intervene and help keep Beverly Hills neat.

I accomplished this by simply bending down and stripping off the small rubber band that encircled the folded newspapers. Now shorn of their protection, the exposed pages were vulnerable to all the elements: rain, wind, lawn sprinklers and lawn mowers.

As I write this I must confess that, since moving into my neighborhood fifty-two years ago, this is the second time, I have acted as a compulsive rubber band stripper. I do not know how many bands I will accumulate from my current stripping sessions, but in my original vigilante raids, I may have appropriated at least a hundred rubber bands. The original 'band' was red, thinner and infinitely more pleasing to the eye than the tan, beige-ish, thicker, less aesthetic ones I am now collecting.

The very first red rubber band I liberated, I put to immediate use and, since that day, I have used a rubber band for the same purpose. I place it around the small wad of the U.S. currency I carry in my pants pocket and use it as a money clip. This light, cheap rubber band replaced the expensive, weighty gold money clip that Sid Caesar had given me as a Christmas gift in 1958.

I think I know where I last saw this money clip and I will now check to see how well my memory still serves me.

I actually got up and discovered that my memory serves me well. I opened a drawer I had not opened in years, and found the gold money clip where I had put it-- under a stack of expired passports, in a box of old cuff links. The money clip, fashioned of real gold, shone as brilliantly as ever. Embossed on it was a bas-relief rendition of the faces of comedy and tragedy.

At this juncture, I stopped writing to greet a welcome visitor who popped into my office. Mel Brooks, who had just lunched with friends in Beverly Hills, had dropped by to say hello. He felt bad that he had interrupted my meanderings and instructed me to continue jotting down things while he catches a few dozen winks on the built-in couch that sits three feet from the desk at which I am sitting. I did not mind one bit as, all through my life, I have always welcomed interruptions. I have heard many writers confess that they not only like to be interrupted but that they live for interruption.

Mr. Brooks' visit could not have come at a better time as I had come to a point in my little tale that had no clear path ahead. After noticing that the gold money clip had a bas-relief of the comedy/tragedy masks, I had nothing more to say—and do you know what?... I am just going to shut up!

Time: One full day later.

I decided to speak again after I was visited by Larry O'Flahavan, the gentleman who helped me shepherd my bio "I Remember Me" from its incarnation to its being published as a hard cover, eBook and iBook. Larry is not only a good friend but an excellent sounding board, and to get his input on my rubber band-money clip story, I read it to him and described my elation at searching for and actually finding the gold money clip I had used to hold my bills before switching to a rubber band. He reacted the way I hoped he would, and we discussed how much more material I was going to add to "I Just Remembered" before I put it to bed. We also discussed, "Ooh, I Almost Forgot!" as an alternate title, but decided that the two bios both having the word "Remember" makes our first choice preferable.

Before Larry left, we discussed the efficacy of putting out an audio book of "I Remember Me." I had recently taped it for our archives and after listening to it, I thought, "Why should I be the only one getting such great pleasure hearing an interesting biography read so well by a well known and, in some quarters, beloved actor?"

After Larry left, I picked up the gold money clip, looked at it carefully and wondered about one aspect of it. Something bothered me when I thought about how I had used that clip to hold paper money. When I showed it to Larry, I had attempted to slip a small wad of money into it but was not able to do so. I struggled and spread open the bottom of the clip about a millimeter before it snapped back and gave the tip of my index finger a painful hickey.

It was a mystery and I actually was bothered by the fact that I could not remember how it was possible to use this expensive gift that Sid Caesar had given me. I absolutely remember once taking a wad of money out of my money clip and snapping a rubber band around it.

I picked up the gold money clip, looked at the smiling and frowning masks of comedy and tragedy and smiled and frowned back at them. Little did I know that, as I made my way back to the chest of drawers to put the money clip back from whence it came, a thought would pop into my head.

Hey Reiner, is it at all possible that there is another gold money clip somewhere in one of these drawers that would clear up this mystery?

With that I dropped the money clip back into its wooden jewelry box, opened another drawer, and found more long lost articles, among them a Yarmulke I had once worn at some bar mitzvah or memorial service, a cigar box that contained mementos from the 1968 George McGovern-Sargent Shriver short lived presidential campaign– the mementos were in the form of gold plated finger rings that spelled out the word McGovern and Shriver.

In that same box, I unearthed the solution to the money-clip mystery. For those of you who guessed that there was another gold money clip, you would have been almost 100% correct. I say almost because you would never guess who had presented me with the clip and who had my initials engraved on it.

It was not Sid Caesar but Perry Como. How had this come about? I had not a clue but I had a computer and access to Google. I Googled Perry Como and Carl Reiner and within ten seconds I had my answer. On his 1956 "The Perry Como Show" Perry had presented gold money clips to a raft of stars who had appeared as his guests– among others, the list included Rosemary Clooney, Frankie Laine, Sid Caesar, Nanette Fabray, Carl Reiner and Howard Morris.

To Carl "Gratefully" -Perry

The mystery was only partly solved; persisting was a niggling detail–the origin of the clip with its embossed comedy and tragedy masks. I spent last evening and a good part of the morning trying to come up with how, where, when and under what circumstances someone gifted me with this solid gold unusable money-clip, and I believe I have come upon the answer. It was my thinking the word "unusable" that triggered the denouement.

It was Sid Caesar who had ordered his assistant to procure and distribute these gold money clips as Christmas presents to the members of his cast and crew. The assistant was proud that he had made a good deal, in getting these clips at 'just a bit above cost.'

I am sure, knowing Sid, that when he discovered the reason he was able to buy these "fakahktah money clips" so cheaply, he railed at his inept assistant and probably advised his cast that whoever needed extra cash, could melt down their clip and sell the gold.

Perry Como

I am glad to have cleared that up, as it is now time for me to go for my daily stroll. I know that along the way, I will be tempted to stoop and retrieve a rubber band that is crying to be retrieved, but at 91 and 1/2, stooping and retrieving is becoming less inviting, less rewarding and increasingly more like a fruitless endeavor.

It is now one full hour later and I am done doing all of the above. I am satisfied that, except for a couple of typos, I have covered everything I ever wanted to write about or anyone ever wanted to read about the subject of throw-away local newspapers, rubber bands and gold money clips.

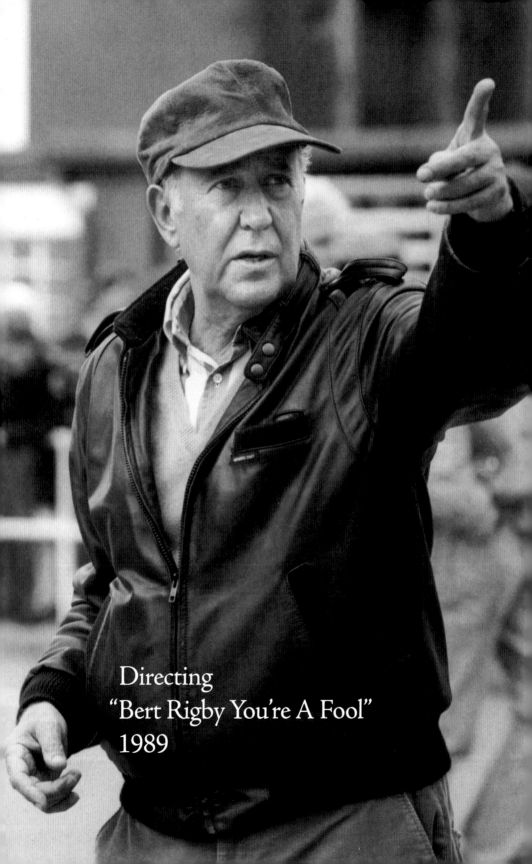

Directing
"Bert Rigby You're A Fool"
1989

The Most Self-Involved Friend I Have

CHAPTER ELEVEN

The Most Self-Involved Friend I Have

I have spent many wakeful hours discussing with myself the pros and cons of putting words to the incident that inspired the above title. I have no doubt that it is a worthy addition to this book, but I do have doubts about the effect its inclusion will have on my relationship with an old "friend"–an old semi-close one would be more accurate. We have known each other for some fifty years, but for the past twenty or so we have seldom dined, lunched, gone to a movie together. He is a good soul and has, I hope, enough of a sense of humor to find this little piece slightly amusing.

The incident occurred what seems a millennium ago, in a land not far from where I now reside. To protect the privacy of this friend I will refer to him as 'this friend.'

The particular day I am about to memorialize was a sunny one in 1989 when I was directing a scene for a movie that I wrote and loved. A few did not, and among the few was Leonard Maltin, who in his Movie Video Guide found it: "...well meaning, silly and contrived." *

This day, that we were shooting a scene for my 'well meaning, silly and contrived' film, which I titled, "Bert Rigby, You're a Fool", was a sunny one. On a tree lined street in Beverly Hills we had set up lights, sound equipment, two cameras and a huge, thirty-foot high camera crane.

The scene involved our star, the versatile British actor, Robert Lindsay, who was playing an English coal miner who fantasizes that he is Fred Astaire.

The scene was based on my having seen the great Fred Astaire going for a stroll down Rodeo Drive, the street where I live. A year or so earlier I had actually followed him just to watch him walk. After dogging him for a couple of blocks I concluded that, in our world, there has never been a more coordinated and graceful human being. I had to restrain myself from applauding.

Fred Astaire

We were, at this moment, in the middle of rehearsing for
cameras and sound, an elaborate musical number. Blaring out of two
large amplifiers was a prerecorded orchestral and voice track of
Robert Lindsey singing "The Continental." Attached to the side
of the film cameras were video cameras that fed the images to the
TV monitors, which allowed me to see what was being shot. I
wore a headset and used a hand mike to converse with my crew. It
was our first full rehearsal, the music was playing, Robert Lindsay
impersonating Fred Astaire, was dancing down the street and
lip-synching to his vocal track.

Robert Lindsay in "Burt Rigby You're A Fool"

George Shapiro and Annie Reiner visit the set.

I was seated on a director's chair and peering at the small monitor when I heard 'this friend' say, "That's a Fred Astaire song! Hey, I knew Fred Astaire! A couple of years ago I had written a song that I knew would be perfect for Fred, so I went to his home and sang it for him-- and he loved it!"

'This friend' went on and on, describing in detail his meeting with "Fred."

It may be hard to believe but not once did 'this friend' seem to notice that I had earphones on my head and was splitting my attention between him and the TV monitor that was in front of us. Not once did he notice or acknowledge the large truck that was parked a few yards from us.

Most people might be curious as to why a truck that had a thirty foot camera crane mounted on it, was parked on his street, or why a song, "The Continental," was blaring from a giant speaker, or why an actor in tails was singing it and dancing up and down his street acting like Fred Astaire.

It may sound as if I am exaggerating but I am not. I have for many years told of this incident. 'This friend' is a most gifted songwriter and his list of hit songs has been recorded by our most esteemed singers. I daresay that, through the years, the music and lyrics of these songs have not only entertained us mightily but have touched our hearts.

'This friend' continues to be a total original. I know of no one who, when bumping into an old friend on the street and asked "How are you?" or "What are you up to these days?" will tell you exactly how he is and what his current projects are. The few times we have bumped into each other, 'this friend' spoke and I listened for long, long, long stretches of time and never, ever did he ask, "How are you, Carl?' and "What are you up to?"

Perhaps, one day, after reading what I have written about him, 'this friend' may find my words instructive. They could make him aware of an unattractive personality quirk he possesses and perhaps inspire him to change–for the better, and he would have done it without having to spend any money on psychoanalysis.

*As to Mr. Maltin's critique: Many reviews that I Googled found "Bert Rigby, You're a Fool" worthy of three stars out of five.

The Poor Peddler And The Carefree Colt

George Tobias

CHAPTER TWELVE

The Poor Peddler And The Carefree Colt

It was the great character actor and comedian, George Tobias, who told me this story about the poor peddler and the crazy horse that pulled a vegetable wagon through the streets of New York.

In 1950 I had the pleasure and pain of appearing with George in a truly mediocre musical comedy revue that was seen by a hapless handful of theatergoers. In December of that year, if you happened to wander into Boston's Shubert Theater, you would have seen this ill-fated, inept show, inaptly titled, "Alive And Kicking." Mercifully, it lived and kicked for a deservedly short life on Broadway, forty-five performances.

When I met George Tobias, he had already enjoyed an enviable career, both in films and on Broadway. He had played major supporting roles in dozens and dozens of Hollywood hits. He supported such actors as Gary Cooper in, "Sergeant York," James Cagney in "Yankee Doodle Dandy, Errol Flynn in "Operation Burma," Bob Hope in "The Seven Little Foys," Jimmy Stewart and June Allyson in "The Glen Miller Story." On Broadway, he had an equally impressive list of plays and parts, and in television, he made, literally, hundreds of appearances on the popular shows of the era.

No Broadway pundit would ever believe that "Alive And Kicking," a show which boasted songs written by the likes of Sammy Fain, Paul Francis Webster and Hoagy Carmichael choreographed by the great Jack Cole and sporting a cast which included, Gwen Verdon, Lenore Lonergan, Jack Gilford, Bobby Van, Jack Cole, Mickey Deems, Fay Dewitt, David Burns, Jack Cassidy, George and myself would close one month after it opened.

I have always had a soft spot in my heart for "Alive and Kicking," for besides meeting and working with extraordinarily talented people, it was the show where, after seeing me perform, producer Max Liebman invited me to join Sid Caesar and Imogene Coca as a cast member of "Your Show Of Shows." I owe a great deal of whatever success I have had to my years with Max, Sid, Imogene and the show.

It was in Boston, during our tryout weeks at the Shubert Theater, that I learned things about and from George Tobias that are etched in my memory.

We lunched together every day and always at a restaurant of his choosing. Directly across from the theater was a celebrated seafood restaurant, whose name I am not sure of but I think it was "The Union Oyster House." What I do remember clearly is George asking me, as we approached the restaurant, if I liked lobster stew. I told him that I loved lobster but I had never had it in a stew. I would never have guessed from his demeanor that he was a sophisticated gourmet. When we arrived at the restaurant, the Maître D' greeted George warmly, as most people did-it seemed that everyone knew and liked George Tobias.

Instead of being escorted to a table, George made his way to the kitchen, pushed open the swinging doors, called out the chef's name and was warmly greeted by him. After introducing me to the chef, George took him aside and had a whispered conversation which ended with George smiling and saying, "Buddy, we only live once!"

While at our table, waiting for our special dish of lobster stew to arrive, George excitedly told me why the stew was so special and why we would have to wait awhile and why "it'll be well worth the wait."

"In our heavenly lobster stew," he explained, "you won't find any lobster tails or claws—you will be eating only lobster knuckles!"

When, a half hour later, the dish arrived, I saw and tasted what George had glowingly described. Floating in a rich, creamy sauce, were dozens of small, succulent nuggets, the lobsters' knuckles. I knew the difficulty I always encountered digging out these tiny taste treasures, and I appreciated how very special and how very expensive was this meal that George Tobias was hosting that night.

Besides being a once-in-a-lifetime taste treat, it was also the night George regaled me with the story of his days working for a fruit peddler and their adventures with a spirited horse.

George had grown up in New York City's lower eastside. In his early teens, before he ever thought of becoming an actor, he worked for a fruit and vegetable peddler–a job he said he enjoyed because, on their rounds, the old vendor would allow him to hold the horse's reins. He told of the horse being a big, beautiful, smart animal that "really knew his way about the city."

"We never had to yank the reins to tell him where to stop." George said, "He had the route memorized. We'd just tap him on his rump and he'd amble to the next stop."

George told how, after a lifetime of dedicated service, the animal passed away, and how devastated his boss was at losing his friend. Sadly, he went out to find his replacement. They visited the stable where he bought the horse that had served him so loyally. The peddler asked the stable owner if it were possible that he would have a horse for sale that was anywhere near as good as the one he had originally sold him.

"You're in luck!" George recalled the owner saying, "Just yesterday, I got a horse on consignment, a beauty! He's smart, strong and for a price that if I asked twice as much, you'd still be getting a bargain."

Assured that the horse was in perfect health, George's boss hitched the animal to the wagon, led him out of the stable and down the street. George said that soon after they turned a corner, the horse, who was calmly ambling along, suddenly picked up his pace and, in a flash, was running full-tilt down the street and directly toward a brick building, which he smashed into head first! Fruits and vegetables were flying about as the horse tumbled to the ground. George said they ran to the fallen animal, unhitched him from the wagon and managed to help the poor beast to his feet. Holding the reins, the angry peddler led the disoriented animal to the stable and demanded the owner return his money. When the owner asked why, the peddler shouted, "Why!? Because you sold me a blind horse!"

"He's not blind!" the owner explained.

"Not blind!!? The horse ran straight into a brick wall!" George yelled, "Don't tell me he's not blind!"

"He's not blind!" the man explained. "He just don't give a fuck!"

George swore to me that what he had just told me was true.

Earlier I alluded to the pain and pleasure of being with the wonderful George Tobias during the out-of-town tryout of "Alive and Kicking." I have described the pleasure George brought me but not the pain I felt for him during rehearsal, as I watched him struggle unsuccessfully to memorize the lines and lyrics he would be saying and singing in the show.

On opening night, when he stepped on stage at the Shubert Theater, an audience who knew and appreciated his talent greeted George with long and heartfelt applause. By the end of the evening his fans did not see the confident, funny and huggable George Tobias, but a man for whom they felt sorry. I don't remember exactly how many performances George gave before David Burns replaced him. We were all sad to see him leave but, for the show to survive, many more things needed to improve. The show had one good sketch, two fair ones, two good songs, seven okay ones and three sensational dancers. The review in the New York Times by Brooks Atkinson, the dean of Broadway critics, praised the performances of David Burns and Jack Gilford, the dancing of Bobby Van, Jack Cole and Valerie Bettis, but summed up by labeling our show: "...a mediocre revue in a mongrel style."

Besides getting to know dear George Tobias, another pleasant memory I have of the show is of my being the 'straight man' for the great comedian, Jack Gilford. We did a sketch where Jack tried desperately to stop smoking. The sketch was funny enough to have a life after the show closed, and we performed it again at New York's legendary Palace Theater. Thanks to the equally legendary Judy Garland, the Palace was refurbished for her one woman show. Judy's show was designed to bring Vaudeville back to Broadway and for a short spell, it did. Following Judy's show, Jack Gilford and I were invited to join a roster of performers and perform our "Smoking Sketch."

For two weeks, we did the fifteen-minute sketch, not once a day or twice a day on matinee days, as we did on Broadway, but six times a day.

After inhaling cigarette smoke six times a day for two weeks I was oh-so-happy that Vaudeville had died.

Jack Gilford

Because I am no longer happy about the demise of Vaudeville, I Googled old acts that once entertained me royally. I became mesmerized by the dozens of clips, bios, articles and memory-laden information about a whole host of great performers but none touched me more than reading about the sad-happy, short, full life of the miraculously talented Judy Garland. I heartily recommend Googling Garland.

Ah, The Sweet Unsolved Mysteries Of My Life

President Franklin D. Roosevelt

CHAPTER THIRTEEN

Ah, The Sweet Unsolved Mysteries Of My Life

There's one mystery that has perplexed me for almost seventy-four years, and which rarely crosses my mind, but when it does, my inner self mumbles, *Why the heck did Barbara Comack dump me?*

I write about it now because a few days ago during my daily around-the-block stroll my inner-ego asked that question.

At seventeen, while working by day as a machinist's helper and a delivery boy of repaired millinery sewing machines, at night I was an actor-in-training. At 6 PM, I would leave Abe Weglinsky's small machine shop at 38th Street and 6th Avenue, travel downtown on the IRT subway to 100 Center Street, where I was studying to become an actor. Thanks to President Franklin D. Roosevelt, who created the NRA (National Recovery Act), which among other things, funded the building of roads, bridges, infra-structures, and supported the fine arts. The lives of many of our nation's great musicians, painters and composers were sustained by what some of our misguided legislators now call "a handout" and, in reality, is a "hand up."

I have written before about how government programs like the WPA (Works Progress Administration) and New York City's National Youth Administration's Radio Workshop were responsible for my career in the performing arts. Those among us who decry that we must "get the government off our backs" have it slightly askew, our government should be offering its back to any of our good citizens to 'get on' should they be in need of food, clothing or shelter.

Before I went 'Tom Paine' on you, I was discussing 100 Center Street, where I enrolled in a free acting class that was overseen by a Mrs. Whitmore. This middle-aged, white-haired woman's pronounced British accent, replete with rolling R's, attested to her pedigree as a classic actress. Her first instruction to the class, in which Barbara Comack and I had enrolled, is one I will never forget, nor will I forget the speech from "Hamlet" that she bid us memorize.

"Class", she said, "as your first assignment, I am going to ask you to do something you may find unusual. I want both the male and female members to learn and deliver a speech from Hamlet! However, I do not want any of Hamlet's soliloquies. No, I want you to learn and perform the speech describing the tragic death of young, naive Ophelia—a speech delivered by Hamlet's mother, Queen Gertrude."

From Mrs. Whitmore's class the two things I took that have stayed with me until now are the mysterious disappearance of Barbara Comack and the words Shakespeare fashioned for Queen Gertrude.

If you were to wake me from a deep sleep and request that I recite Gertrude's speech, you will hear:

"There is a willow grows aslant a brook that shows its hoar leaves in the glassy stream. There with fantastic garlands did she come, with crow flowers, nettles, daisies and long purples that liberal shepherds give a grosser name—but our cold maids do dead men's fingers call them—There, upon a coronet clambering to hang, an envious sliver broke, when down her weedy trophies and herself, fell into the weeping brook...her clothes spread wide and mermaid-like whilst they bore her up, at which time she chanted snatches of old tunes, as one incapable of her own distress...soon her clothes, heavy with drink, pulled the poor wretch from her melodious lay to muddy death."

I will not stand behind the accuracy of the above but for seven decades, whenever I recall my days at Mrs. Whitmore's acting class, those are the words that pour out of me.

It was during my days at 100 Center Street that Mrs. Whitmore assigned a young actress, Barbara Comack, to read a scene with me from Hamlet. We did well enough to impress Mrs. Whitmore, who recommended us to a producer-director-playwright, who had come to monitor her class. He was preparing to mount an off-off-off Broadway production and had Barbara and myself read a short love scene from his play.

I remember nothing about the play but I clearly remember falling in love with this pretty, blonde-haired, sweet smelling girl who, for a love scene, had been directed to sit on my lap.

I do not recall this producer's name but I do recall his taking Barbara and me to a seedy rehearsal hall where we rehearsed a short scene from his badly written experimental play. Our relationship with this director-producer and his play ended in less than a week.

My time spent in Mrs. Whitmore's acting class lasted less than two months, but my relationship with Barbara Comack lasted almost a full year, and a romantically blissful year it was. We managed to spend as much time together as we could. Her mother was totally amenable to her daughter and me sitting on the couch in the living room of her Bronx apartment. She seemed to enjoy hearing us chatter about the theater, our place in it and how someday we might go to a summer theater and, together, perform in plays or musicals.

We so enjoyed ourselves when we impersonated Jeanette MacDonald and Nelson Eddy and belted out the song, "I'll See You Again" from Noel Coward's operetta, "Bitter Sweet."

Nelson Eddy and Jeannette MacDonald in "Bittersweet"

When her mother was not present we managed to get in some mild smooching that consisted of tight hugs and tongue-less kissing. I being all of seventeen and a half and she having just turned sweet sixteen, were nowhere near getting engaged, but we spoke of the possibility—especially after midway through our relationship when, for a brief moment, I dared to fondle her bosom.

Barbara lived in an upscale Bronx apartment building off the elegant Grand Concourse and I lived in a crumbling tenement on the proverbial,'other side of the tracks.' After a day of working as a delivery boy, an evening of appearing onstage at the Gilmore Theater and a late night smooching session with Barbara Comack, the dull ache in my groin made my nightly long walk home a painful experience.

By the end of the year, I was so deeply in love and committed to Barbara that I wanted only to share with her all the exciting things I knew, including my knowledge of The Bronx Zoo. The Zoo was a place that from infant-hood, my parents, in lieu of sending my brother Charlie and me to a camp, took us to this great animal sanctuary.

At 17 with an enhanced pencil moustache

I knew every nook and cranny of the great park and where all the most unusual and entertaining animals were housed. I had hand-fed the camels, llamas and goats and had actually witnessed a lengthy head-to-head horn-butting contest between the King of the big horned goats and a younger goat that challenged the Chief's ability to lead the herd.

I was terribly excited the Saturday morning I had made a date to escort Barbara Comack to my Bronx Park. I had put on my best slacks and jacket and was ready to entertain and impress my steady girl. I was just about to leave my folks' apartment, when the phone rang. It was Barbara, and before I could tell her how excited I was about our forthcoming outing, she informed me that she had to call off our date as a cousin of hers had just arrived from Connecticut. That was it! Before I could ask if we could reschedule our date for the following day, Sunday, she coldly informed me that it would be best if I did not try to contact her again! I heard a loud click and an even louder silence. I thought of re-dialing her number but the finality and the coldness with which she delivered her message discouraged me—forever.

All that day, all that night and for the next few weeks, I wondered what in the world had soured our relationship. I thought and thought but could not come up with any clue that made sense. I finally decided that it was not Barbara's cousin that was visiting from Connecticut but Barbara's old boyfriend. I concluded that when her interest in him was reborn, her ardor for me died.

A few months after our break-up, I sent Barbara a postcard informing her that I was a resident member of the Rochester Summer Stock Company. A week later I received a card from her with a short congratulatory note.

And there is where I left it seventy-four years ago, and since then I have discovered nothing more about Barbara Comack's motive for summarily dumping me. It remains one of niggling, albeit persistent, not so sweet mysteries of my life.*

*Yes, I did Google Barbara Comack's name with no success.

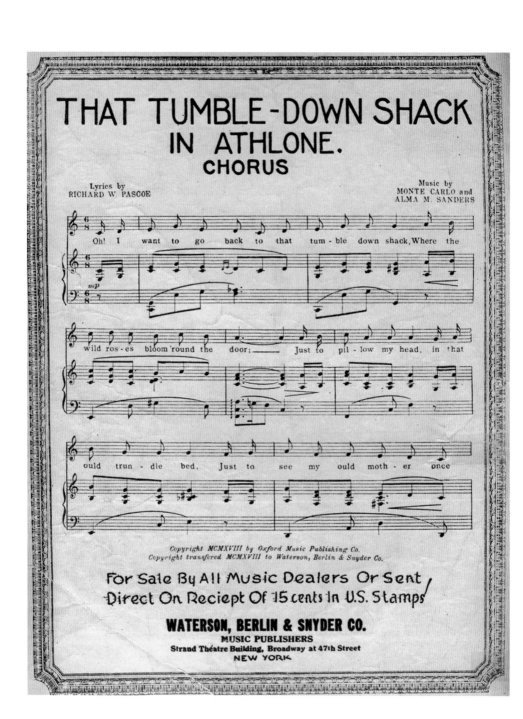

THAT TUMBLE-DOWN SHACK
IN ATHLONE.
CHORUS

Lyrics by
RICHARD W. PASCOE

Music by
MONTE CARLO and
ALMA M. SANDERS

Oh! I want to go back to that tum-ble down shack, Where the wild ros-es bloom 'round the door; Just to pil-low my head, in that ould trun-dle bed, Just to see my ould moth-er once

WATERSON, BERLIN & SNYDER CO.
MUSIC PUBLISHERS
Strand Théatre Building, Broadway at 47th Street
NEW YORK

How, In Just Thirty Days, I Learned All
The Lyrics To A Very Short Song

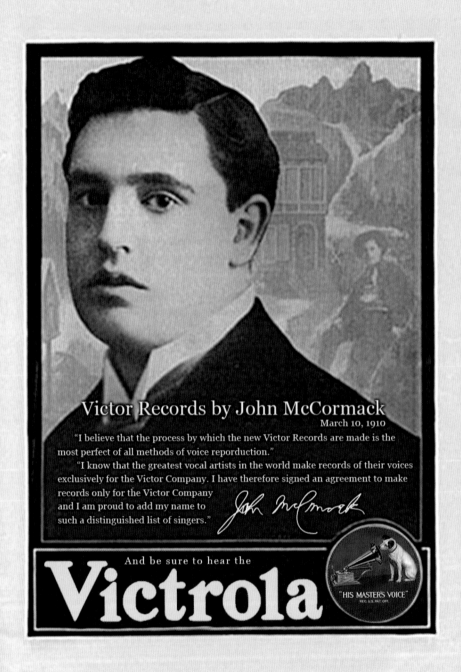

CHAPTER FOURTEEN

How, In Just Thirty Days, I Learned All The Lyrics To A Very Short Song

Most people might find that I am being crassly self-serving when I again reference myself. In chapter forty-seven of my informative and entertaining 2013 autobiography, "I Remember Me," I wrote about Judy Garland and my love of the classic Irish song, "That Tumble Down Shack In Athlone." I have loved that song since I was about eight. I had heard an Irish tenor, John McCormack, sing it on an RCA Victor recording and I wanted to be him. To that end I learned some of the lyrics and sang them with an Irish brogue. Well, thirty days ago, for some reason, I found myself humming that tune and trying to remember the lyrics. I had forgotten all but the first two lines. I shut my eyes and tried hard to contact the part of my brain that stores old, memorized song lyrics, but no luck. Nothing came to me but the first two lines of that sixteen line song. I needed to memorize those elusive fourteen others. I wondered why I was so obsessed about memorizing the lyrics to "The Tumble Down Shack In Athlone," and as soon as I asked myself that question, the answer, as if it was spring-loaded, came back at me, *If I ever go on a late night show and tell them about why, when I was eight years old, I wanted to be an Irish tenor, I'd sing the song.*

Of the missing sixteen lines of the "Tumble Down Shack" I have locked in a little more than half, but the struggle goes on. I am determined to be ready if and when I am again asked to sing.

It was in my physical therapist's office, five sessions ago, I had started the process of learning that old favorite. To that end, I brought with me a two inch square of paper which had printed on it a computer-Googled, tiny-lettered copy of the song's lyrics.

It was with hot packs on my back and neck, while lying alone on the trainer's table for ten minutes, that I struggled to memorize the words, trying hard not to peek too often at the tiny-lettered paper. And finally—finally my doggedness paid off.

"HOOOOOOORRRRRRRAAAAAAAAAAYYYYYYYY" was the word that echoed through my head after that session and all the way home. It was there, while lying on the heating pads, I correctly sang all the lyrics of "That Tumble Down Shack In Athlone," and I did it without once glancing at my paper.

At that moment, whether or not on one of the late night shows, I got to exhibit 'me foine brogue' singing: "Jes to pillow me head in me auld trumble bed, jes to see me dear Mither once more..."

I am no longer a frustrated singer but a very content senior citizen!

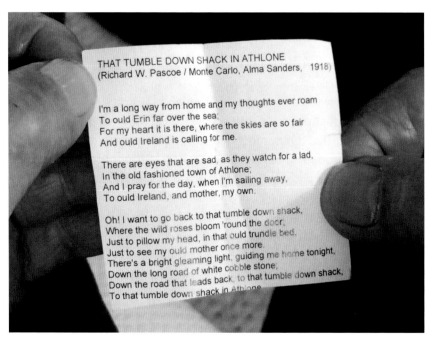

"That Tumble Down Shack In Athlone"
by Pascoe, Carlo & Sanders 1918

Rehearsing "That Tumble Down Shack In Athlone"

Solo B♭ Trumpet

Per il mio amico Jens Lindemann

VESTI LA GIUBBA
from I Pagliacci

R. Leoncavallo
(1857-1919)
Arranged by David Marlatt

To Pass Time Faster I Sing My Arias Slower

Carl Reiner (Left), Charlie Reiner (Right) with my mother Bessie Reiner

CHAPTER FIFTEEN

To Pass Time Faster I Sing My Arias Slower

I thank whatever stars are guiding me through this, my ninety first year on earth. I am so pleased that my body is still capable of casting a shadow. My bi-weekly physical therapy ministrations have kept me relatively hale and mobile. For most of the hour session, a therapist will be at my side, massaging all the knots and kinks in my spine and lower back and helping me to stretch muscles that need to be stretched.

A needed relaxing moment comes when I lie on a torso length heating pad and have a small hot pack strapped to my neck. The therapist leaves me alone for ten minutes—and tells me that if I need him, I can ring the little bell he left on a side table.

Ten minutes can be a long time, especially if you have nothing to think about but the fact that you are going to be lying there for ten boring minutes. As a youngster, my mother used two Yiddish phrases to describe me. She accused me of having 'shpilkes en tuchus,' (splinters in my ass). Harboring this trait would make my ten minute wait seem like an eternity...unless I came up with an antidote, which I did. "Vesti La Giubba," the aria from "Pagliacci," popped into my head. I knew that the aria was a short one but I wondered if I could sing it at a tempo that would make it last for most of the ten minutes I had to kill. I checked my watch and, giving each word its musical due, I started to mouth the aria's Italian words:

Recitaaaar! Mentro preeeeesso dal deliiiirio,Non so pi quel che dico e quel che faccio! Eppur duopo sfooooorzati, Bah! Sei tu forse un uooooooom--Tu se' Palgiacciiiiii! Vesti la guibbaaaa, e la facciaaaa infarinaaaa. La gente pagaaa e rider vuole quaaaaaa. Eeee seeee Arlecchiiiiin tinvola Coloooombinaaaa, ridi Pagliaaaaacciiiiii, e ognuuuun applaudiiiir! Traaaamuuuuta in lazzi lo spaaaasmo ed il piantoooo, In uuuuna smorfiaaaa il singhiozzooooo deeeel dolooooor Ahhhhhhhhh! Ridiiiiiii Pagliaaaaaacciiiiii, sui tuo aaaaaaamooooore infraaaantooo, Ridi del duaaaal che taveeeelenaaaa il coooooooor.

As the last note faded, I checked and discovered that less than two minutes had elapsed. Now I knew what I had to do: Sing at a slower tempo that would allow me to fill up the remaining eight minutes–and I succeeded, singing it twice, once at three minutes and forty seconds and once at four minutes.

I am aware of how nuttily compulsive my behavior may sound, but if you ever get into a position similar to what I have outlined, you would do well to have a song ready to sing or a poem ready to recite to yourself –both excellent ways for whiling away time.

Two days after whiling away time singing Pagliacci, I learned from my manager, George Shapiro, that I had been invited to appear on Conan O'Brien's television show. I was still in the process of promoting the sales of my recently published biography, "I Remember Me," and I was excited about the possibility of doing something on his show that I had never dared to do on any of the talk shows I had visited in the past fifty years, sing " Vesti La Giubba".

I was relatively secure that I could sing a credible on-key and in rhythm version of Leoncavallo's "Vesti La Giubba." I had done just that about a month earlier when being released from Cedar's Sinai Hospital after an overnight stay. I had had a bad bout with a dehydrating virus that I thought would do me in. I was so happy to be told by the floor nurse that I was going to be discharged that day that I broke into song....or rather 'into aria.' I belted a tolerable, on-key, in rhythm version of "Vesti La Giubba," that had the ward nurse thanking me for making her day. She actually said, "Mr. Reiner you have just made my day!"

So when on Conan O'Brien's Show, Conan asked: "Carl, is there anything in show business you have not done that you would like to have done?" I answered, "I would love to have been an opera singer."

I explained that I have always sung in Broadway shows and on television's "Your Show Of Shows" but my operatic singing was always comic in nature. I had a strong voice with a three octave range but lacked a couple of things that made opera an unlikely vocation for me; I often sang off key and out of rhythm. But I would love to sing the aria, if he would allow me. Conan allowed and I sang.

It may sound immodest but that night's performance was more than I had ever hoped for, but you do not have to rely on my assessment.

My operatic debut

You have but to turn on your computers, Google the September 5th, 2013 Conan O'Brien Show and judge for yourself. For those of you who do not use a computer or simply don't care to make the effort, I will cull some of what was reported about my work on that night.

"Carl Reiner, you have gone viral! Your performance of Pagliacci on Conan last night is all over the internet, YouTube and numerous other sites, which includes the promotion of your memoir, "I Remember Me," and its iBook.

"Carl Reiner's singing Vesti La Giubba on Conan's show was fantastic. Amazing at 91 years!"

"LOVED Reiner's performance, it was infused with energy!"

The positive comment about my singing by a head nurse at Cedars Sinai and the healthy applause I received from Conan's audience are enough to keep me smiling until at least October. In researching the lyrics of Vesti La Giubba, I ran across some information that may be of interest to you, if you ever wondered, as I have, who were some of the world's great operatic tenors who sang their version of "Vesti La Giubba" before I joined their ranks. Here are their names: *Enrico Caruso, Richard Tucker, Beniamino Gigli, Mario Lanza, Leo Slezak, Jussi Bjorling, Jan Peerce, Jose Carreras, Placido Domingo, Tito Schipa, Carlos Bergonzi, Mario Del Monaco, Lauritz Melchior, Giuseppe De Stefano, Robert Hostalvy, Joseph Calleja and Alfredo Kraus.*

Johnny Carson

47 Real Appearances with Johnny Carson
and 3 Fake Ones

Three of my real appearances on
Johnny Carson's Tonight Show.

CHAPTER SIXTEEN

48 Real Appearances With Johnny Carson and 2 Fake Ones

The late-night talk shows, circa B.C. (Before Carson), were hosted by some of our most gifted performers. The original host of NBC's "The Tonight Show" was the multi-talented musician-comedian, Steve Allen, who was at the helm from 1954 until 1957. He was followed by the charming, witty and empathetic Jack Paar, who reigned for five years until his tearful retirement in 1962. Johnny Carson came on that year and held court for thirty entertainment packed years before making a touching farewell speech and riding off into the sunset.

I daresay that all of our current and talented television hosts would agree that Johnny Carson set the template for how a late night 'talk show' should be conducted.

Then, as now, any actor, director, producer who wished to plug their latest project, was more than pleased to be booked for an appearance on Johnny's show.

Year after year, "The Tonight Show" bracketed hours of light-hearted interviews and serious conversations with great entertainment which often showcased budding musical or comedic talents.

Watching one of Johnny's farewell shows, I learned that Tony Randall, the beloved Broadway and television star, who was the main guest that night, was making his seventy-fifth appearance on Johnny's show!

It is one record that will never be broken, or even approached.

Tony Randall (Feb. 26, 1920-May 17, 2004)

On April 28th, 1992, during the last month of his thirty year run, I was invited to appear for a farewell visit. That night I was one of three guests, the others being, the blues legend B. B. King and an upcoming, young comedian Jerry Seinfeld. Not too long before, when hosting a cable show featuring young comedians, I, with my my keen sense of comedy predicted that this young, handsome lad would one day become THE Jerry Seinfeld, one of the icons of American comedy and Host of the tremendously popular "Comedians In Cars Getting Coffee which he graciously invited myself and Mel Brooks to make a guest appearances. I can't tell you how many strangers have come up to me and said that our appearance on Jerry's new show might be one of the reasons that he won The 2013 Webby Award for Outstanding Comedy Performance!

Jerry Seinfeld and Johnny Carson, April 24, 1992

So that memorable night on Johnny's show I came on as I always did, dancing wildly until the audience laughed and applauded, which to spare me a heart attack, they always did.

I mentioned to Johnny that I had seen Tony Randall boast of his seventy-fifth appearances with him and I felt bad that my forty-eight was a sorry, distant second. I said I would have loved to be able to include in my resume that I had been on Johnny's show fifty times. 'Fifty', I pleaded, "is a nice round number, much more impressive than forty-eight."

On the air, without discussing this before the show, I asked Johnny if he would accommodate my quirk by introducing me two more times, which bless him, he did. Each time he introduced me I dashed out of the wings, did my wild dance, sat down, exchanged a few pleasantries with him, then darted off. For my second entrance, I returned carrying my jacket and while dancing, I used it as a toreador's cape. I am thankful to my good friend Johnny for all the laughs he afforded me during his thirty year reign on NBC's "The Tonight Show".

To me Johnny Carson is still the King of Late Night!

Cark Reimer

This Here Book...

FOREWORD BY
**WILLY
CRYSTAL**

Preface

The reason why this, my seventh novel, is attributed to Cark Reimer and not Carl Reiner is, I think worth noting. Those of you who type, are aware that on all typewriter and computer keyboards, the L and K keys are side by side and I, being a mediocre typist, have, more often than not, misspelled my name by hiting the wrong key. I did it again today, however this time instead of correcting it, I realized that I had inadvertently given myself an exciting opportunity.

In my recent autobiography, "I Remember Me", I was naturally its' central character, and now, I could be the focal point of an exciting romance-adventure novel about the life and times of a quasi-fictional character named Cark and, substituting an m for the n in Reiner, I became **Cark Reimer.**

"I was so pleased that Cark asked me to write the Foreword for this book and so happy that I did have the time to do it."

-Willy Crystal

"At last a book easy to memorize."

-Nick Van Dyke

"Cark is a tad handsomer than me and I'm not jealous."

-Jorge Clooney

"I love the sexy way Cark Reimer makes single entendres sound like double ones."

-Cara Silverman

"Brevity and levity."

-Saul Reiser

"I never expected a 3-page book to hold my interest so intensely

-Will Maher

"Even though Cark Reimer's book is but 3 pages long, I couldn't put it down."

-Mal Brooks

"I read Cark's book twice and loved it more the second time. Looking forward to a third time."

-Jersey Seinfeld

"Kept me totally entertained for 4 minutes and 15 seconds."

-Talbert Brooks

"Cark's book is well worth a penny."

-Ray Leno

"Finally, the ultimate toilet book."

-Timmy Kimmel

THIS HERE BOOK...
by
CARK REIMER

RANDOM
CONTENT
PUBLISHING

RANDOM CONTENT
Beverly Hills, CA 90210
www.RandomContent.com
Phone: + 1 555.588.2275
carkreiner@randomcontent.com

Published by Random Content 04/22/14

"Inviting people to laugh at you while you are laughing at yourself is a good thing to do. You may be the fool but you are the fool in charge."

-CARL REINER "MY ANECDOTAL LIFE" 2003
-CARL REINER "I REMEMBER ME" 2013

Acknowledgement

I will forever be beholden to my literary friends who volunteered to write a Foreword and to contribute the blurbs for "This Here Book…"

Foreword

FORWARD!

-Willy Crystal

Here now is the genesis of my then untitled new work. As I settled into bed that night, three titles for the book popped into my head: "Cark's Last Lark", "Carksism Versus Marxism" and "The Mark Of Cark!" Three decidedly unsatisfactory titles to be sure. I also discarded "No Reimer Or Reason" but just as I was about to nod off, the perfect title bubbled up and I jotted it down.

"This Here Book That You Hold In Your Hands And That You Just Purchased Is The Most Satisfying And The Last Book You Will Ever Need to Read For It Fully Encompasses Everything Worth Reading From Elizabethan And Renaissance Classics To Steamy Modern Romance And Adventure Novels, Scientific Journals, Collections Of Modern And Ancient Poetry, Adroit Political Essays, Transcendental Meditation, The 'World Atlas, Both The Farmer's and Poor Richard's Almanacs, The Holy Bibles of All Established Religions, The European, Asian And American Medical Journals, The Psychiatric Papers of Drs. Sigmund Freud, Karl Jung, Melanie Klein And Wilfred Bion. The Most Important Editorials From The Pages Of The New York Times, The London Times, The Wall Street Journal, USA Today, The New York Daily News, News And World Report, The Huffington Post, Vanity Fair, The New York Post, The Post Times At All Racetracks, The Monthly AARP, The Weekly Beverly Hills Courier, News of Celebrity Pairings as Reported In The National Enquirer, People, Us, Ebony, Time Magazine, And The Diet and Nutritional Guides Of Nutri-System, Weight Watchers, The Pritikin Center, Jenny Craig, and The Official Handbook For The Cure and Treatment of All Eating Disorders, Including Bulimia, Anorexia, and Morbid Obesity"

I asked myself if it was good title and quickly decided that it was not a good title—it was a great and original title! A fast count made me realize that at one-hundred-and-ninety-nine words, I had written the longest book title in the history of literature. I thought,

"This little baby is a cinch to be included in the next edition "The Guinness Book Of Records"—may even be used as a question on "Jeopardy".

For a brief moment I worried that people who wish to buy the book won't be able to remember the title, but I realized that as soon as someone asks for the book with the long title, the clerk will know it's Cark Reimer's.

"Yeah", I thought," Now all I have to do is write the darned thing". I thought of our public library whose shelves were crowded with the works of Tolstoy, Dostoevsky, Faulkner, Dreiser, Lewis, Salinger, Hardy Dickinson, Austin, Eliot, Roth, Wolf ,Twain, Dickens, Shakespeare and told myself:

"Hey Cark, these literary giants used up all the great plots, all the exciting characters, and every human involvement that ever existed–those word-hogs used every damned word that ever existed–they left me with nothing to write "This Here Book" with-- and I am sure none of them ever ended a sentence with 'with'. All I can boast about is having written the longest title for a book that I have not written. –Hey, for the longest title ever written, how about I write the shortest novel ever written–a ten page romance novel! In all of literature no author has ever written a ten page novel—and if someone has, I'll bet no one ever wrote an engrossing seven page one–or-better yet, an engrossing three pager! That's it! A 198 word titled, three page semi-auto biographical romance novel by Cark Reimer that depicts his struggles... no not his struggles, MY struggles as a... a... a what? An actor, a lawyer ...or...or, I know an obese man! That's it! A very obese Cark Reimer who loses weight and finds love. Perfect! If I start now I could write a page or more before dinner and if I work through dinner, I'll be able to finish the book before Conan's show goes on!"

I ordered a Domino's pizza and started writing. I wolfed down four wedges and finished the last page in time to watch Conan O'Brien's opening monologue. Here now, is the three page romance novel, who's title is 199 words long:

THIS HERE BOOK...

Page One

Two years ago in Provo, Utah, at the "Rehabilitation Center For Life Threatening Eating Disorders," Cark Reimer met Carla Rheemer. They bore similar names but had dissimilar problems. Earlier Cark had toyed with the idea of enrolling at the Center but decided to wait until he reached a weight where he felt out of control. He felt in control at four hundred pounds but when he topped out at five hundred and ten pounds, he taxied to the train station and purchased three coach seats to Provo.

Carla Rheemer had been on a stringent diet before arriving at the Center. She was hoping to lose at least nine pounds from her five feet, eight inch frame. Her target weight was a trim sixty-five pounds. Carla had always prided herself on being a sensible eater.

"I only eat when I am hungry," she would explain, "so many people eat whether they are hungry or not. I am just one of the lucky ones who never gets hungry. If ever I feel faint, I will munch on the one of two soda crackers I aways keep in my pocket or purse."

The day when Carla fainted four times, is the day her father and step-mother arranged for an ambulance to drive her to the "Center For Life Threatening Eating Disorders."

Cark Reimer and Carla Rheemer's first encounter at the Center was at breakfast and Cark's first words to Carla were, "Miss, are you going to eat that roll?" And Carla's to Cark were, "No, you can have it—and my banana, orange juice, Cheerios and this carton of whole milk—I'll keep my glass of water."

For the rest of that first week, Cark managed to sit next to Carla at every meal. Their verbal exchanges were sparse and consisted mainly of Carla offering Cark whatever food was on her plate and Cark happily accepting it.

Surprisingly, their most profoundly bonding moment came, not in the dining room, but in the Center's library. The two stood at the desk of the librarian, Ms. Marian and unwittingly in unison, asked, "Would you happen to have copy of Cark Reimer's "This Here Book....?"

"Ten dozen copies arrived last night," Ms. Marian replied, "and thanks to the rave reviews, they just flew off the shelves. I have not read it but from it's very, very long title and the information on the flap, it seems to be some sort of self-help book. We have but two copies left."

Cark and Carla each checked out a copy. I believe it is safe to say that no two people ever gained more from the simple act of borrowing a book from a public library than Carla Rheemer and Cark Reimer did.

Page Three

Cark Reimer, the five-hundred-ten pound rotunda of a man, is now a muscularly sculpted Adonis who tips the scales at 175 pounds.

Carla Rheemer added 64 lbs to her targeted weight of her 64 lbs and is now a curvaceous 128 lb beauty.

In January, 2013: Two years after their arrival, Cark Reimer and Carla Rheemer successfully ended their treatment.

In March, 2014: Carla Rheemer gave her hand in marriage to the new owner of The Provo Rehabilitation Center and became Mrs. Carla Rheemer-Reimer.

In June, 2015: Mrs. Carla Rheemer-Reimer delivered the first of ten children.

In May, 2047: Four medals of freedom were presented to Cark & Carla Rheemer-Reimer by the thirty-two year old Signora Consuela Rheemer-Reimer-Longoria, our nation's **SECOND WOMAN PRESIDENT** of the **UNITED STATES.***

The End

*In January 2017: **FIRST WOMAN PRESIDENT** Hillary Rodham Clinton
being congratulated during Inaugural Address by outgoing President Barack Obama
as **FIRST MAN** William Jefferson Clinton 'kvells'.

William Shakespeare (April 23, 1564-April 23, 1616)

Shakespeare Misspoke, The Play Is Not
The Thing, The Audience Is The Thing!

CHAPTER EIGHTEEN

Shakespeare Misspoke, The Play Is Not The Thing, The Audience Is The Thing!

In the mid-1960's, my wife and I attended a premiere performance of a new Broadway play. I do not recall its title, but I do remember how mediocre it was and how it triggered me to write a play. Up until now, that one-act, multi-scene play, "Shakespeare Misspoke, The Play Is Not The Thing, The Audience Is The Thing!" which I am proud to have authored, has been lying in the bottom draw of my desk waiting for someone to rescue it. If not I, then who will bring to life this brilliant chef d'oeuvre?

I am aware that describing something I wrote as 'brilliant' makes me appear egotistical, but I am certain that if you could read or see this play you would conclude that I was not being immodest but rather self-effacing.

As I said, I do not remember the title of the play that inspired me that night but I do remember that seated in the audience were a number of well known celebrities.

Soon after the curtain went up, actually in the very first scene, it became apparent that the play, even though it was performed by very good actors, was not worth the effort they were expending. The play's leading characters were less than scintillating, and when the curtain came down on the first act, I whispered to my wife:

"You know, in this audience, there must be dozens of people whose lives are more interesting than those characters onstage—and we'd probably be better entertained if we were listening to their stories."

During the course of the play, I kept thinking about what I had said to Estelle, and I kept thinking about it on the ride back to our hotel and on our flight back to L.A.

Not long after, I sat at my computer and wrote something that I believe is one of the most original things I have ever written... maybe the most original.

Going with the premise that the stories and familial involvements that members of a theater audience have, are very likely to be good material on which to build a play, I did just that. I decided that the paying audience, who would naturally be seated in an auditorium, would be watching a play that took place onstage, a stage that had as its set, a theater auditorium. To give the audience a clearer view of the actors, they would perform on a raked stage, much like the bleachers in a baseball stadium. The play's dialogue would be culled from the conversations and remarks that members of the audience have while filtering into the theater and settling into their seats.

From the audience's tidbits and the instructions from a stage manager, who asks that we turn off our cell phones, a 17 character play emerged, an actor-audience interactive play, that among other things, celebrated the birth of the great art of Pantomime. Yes Pantomime, a presently maligned art form that, I postulate, originated on a fifty-five square mile peninsula aptly named Pantomimmia.

For those of you who are curious about when and where you can see and experience this innovative theatrical experience, I am happy to say that I have just called Michael Ritchie, the artistic director of the Los Angeles Center Theater Group, overseeing The Mark Taper Forum. Hopefully in the next few months or within a year two, he will agree that "Shakespeare Misspoke, The Play Is Not The Thing, The Audience Is The Thing!" is worthy of being scheduled for production at this vaunted Center. If this happens, the entire theater world will reap untold pleasure and I, if lucky, residual benefits.

How I Learned 'YouTube' Is Not 'HisTube,' 'HerTube,' 'YourTube,' 'Their Tube,' Or 'Anybody Else In The Entire World's Tube,' 'But My Tube'

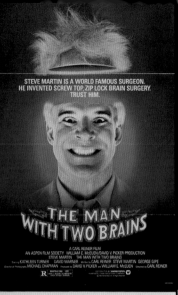

STEVE MARTIN IS A WORLD FAMOUS SURGEON.
HE INVENTED SCREW TOP, ZIP LOCK BRAIN SURGERY.
TRUST HIM.

THE MAN WITH TWO BRAINS

AN ASPEN FILM SOCIETY · A CARL REINER FILM
WILLIAM E. McEUEN/DAVID V. PICKER PRODUCTION
STEVE MARTIN · THE MAN WITH TWO BRAINS
KATHLEEN TURNER · DAVID WARNER · CARL REINER · STEVE MARTIN · GEORGE GIPE
MICHAEL CHAPMAN · DAVID V. PICKER and WILLIAM E. McEUEN · CARL REINER

They say that behind every great man there's a woman.
But in this case it's ridiculous.

STEVE MARTIN · LILY TOMLIN
ALL OF ME
The comedy that proves that one's a crowd.

A CARL REINER FILM
"Oh, God!"

Opening Soon.

FATAL instinct
A killer comedy.

STEVE MARTIN

LAUGH, OR I'LL BLOW YOUR LIPS OFF ...

A CARL REINER FILM
DEAD MEN DON'T WEAR PLAID

AN ASPEN FILM SOCIETY
WILLIAM E. McEUEN
DAVID V. PICKER PRODUCTION
STEVE MARTIN IN
"DEAD MEN DON'T WEAR PLAID"
RACHEL WARD · RENI SANTONI · CARL REINER
CARL REINER · GEORGE GIPE · STEVE MARTIN
MICHAEL CHAPMAN · MIKLOS ROZSA · EDITH HEAD
BUD MOLIN · DAVID V. PICKER · WILLIAM E. McEUEN
CARL REINER · A UNIVERSAL PICTURE

FILMED IN DETECTO VISION

BERT RIGBY
YOU'RE A FOOL

JOHN CANDY IS ABOUT TO FACE THE MOST DEVASTATING EXPERIENCE
KNOWN TO MAN—THE FAMILY VACATION.

Summer Rental
LIFE IS A BEACH.

PARAMOUNT PICTURES PRESENTS A BERNIE BRILLSTEIN PRODUCTION · A CARL REINER FILM
JOHN CANDY · SUMMER RENTAL · RICHARD CRENNA
MUSIC BY ALAN SILVESTRI · EXECUTIVE PRODUCER BERNIE BRILLSTEIN
WRITTEN BY JEREMY STEVENS & MARK REISMAN · PRODUCED BY GEORGE SHAPIRO
DIRECTED BY CARL REINER · A PARAMOUNT PICTURE

The tush* scene alone
is worth the price of admission.

*That part of the anatomy covered by the stamp.

2 Tush Scene · 2 Tush Scene
2 Tush Scene · 2 Tush Scene
A Commemorative Stamp
Nº 00000

GEORGE SEGAL · RUTH GORDON
"Where's Poppa?"
RON LEIBMAN · TRISH VAN DEVERE
Screenplay by ROBERT KLANE based on novel "Where's Poppa?"
Produced by JERRY TOKOFSKY and MARVIN WORTH
Directed by CARL REINER · United Artists

KIRSTIE ALLEY

SHE DID IT.

AND BOY,
IS SHE SORRY.

SIBLING RIVALRY

How I Learned 'YouTube' Is Not 'HisTube,' 'HerTube,' 'YourTube,' 'Their Tube,' Or 'Anybody Else In The Entire World's,' 'But My Tube'

You are aware, if you have read Chapter 16, that I have written a three page romance novel that sports a one-hundred-and-ninety-nine word title, which I claim is a Guiness Book of Records type world's record for long titles. In keeping with my obsession with skewered literary-titling, I now offer a two page essay on the subject outlined in my top heavy, twenty five word title.

When I was a guest on the Conan O'Brien show and he allowed me to sing "Vesti La Giubba," I YouTubed the names of all the other great tenors before me who sang that aria, and along with that info, it also coughed up a long, long, long documentary-type program that listed everything I had ever done on television. It outlined every show on which I appeared, from 1947 to now. As I watched images of me appearing as a young man, a maturing man, a middleaged man, and as a 91 year old man, I thought: '*Hey, that was a most entertaining evening and, at times, a touching one.*'

Seeing myself cavort in beloved, old television shows alongside my wonderful colleagues, and being told that audiences enjoyed watching us cavort, I thought:

Thanks to whomever came up with a thing called 'YouTube,' I am having a great old time reliving some of the best years of my theatrical life.

It was then I, conceited ass that I am, decided that "YouTube" was invented with me in mind and it does not bother me that millions of others make use of it. You see now why I look upon "YouTube" as being "My Tube!"

Here you can see now why I look upon "YouTube" as being "My Tube!"

149

How To Wisely Use The Hairs
On Your Balding Head

General Douglas MacArthur

CHAPTER TWENTY

How To Wisely Use The Hair
On Your Balding Head

The following memory of an incident that played out in the office of my literary agent, Harry Kalcheim, was triggered by an unsolicited script I received in the morning mail.

The year was 1960 and I was meeting with a talented, young writer, Marvin Worth, who wished to submit a script for me to consider using for an episode of "The Dick Van Dyke Show." Harry Kalcheim represented the young, balding Marvin Worth, who handed me a script and asked if I would read it. Both he and Mr. Kalcheim were surprised when I refused to read it. When asked why I would not read his script, I explained, "Because I don't trust him."

"What makes you say that?" The balding writer asked.

"The way you comb your hair," I said, smiling.

"What's wrong with the way I comb my hair?" he grimaced.

"You're combing it to hide your baldness, it's dishonest."

"General MacArthur didn't think so."

"He must have. We're discussing it. But I can help you."

"How?"

"The way I once helped another young comedy writer who worked on "Your Show Of Shows." I'll show you, if you allow me to demonstrate!"

The young writer gave me permission and, armed with my comb and the pair of scissors I found on Mr. Kalcheim's desk, I began.

First I cut off all the long, comb-over hairs that barely covered his balding pate, then I neatly trimmed and sculpted both his sideburns, and I finished by combing the remaining hairs to lie on his head the way nature had intended for them to lie. I told him that, "By combing it the way you do, people are drawn to notice you are balding."

Marvin gave me permission to do my thing and when I was done he peered into a mirror and looked at himself quizzically. He was not sure what he thought, until Mr. Kalcheim, his agent, told him how much better he looked. He then begrudgingly smiled and thanked me for "the free haircut."

I pointed out the big plus this "free haircut" accomplished.

"Marvin," I said, "now, when you're chatting with a producer or studio head, they will no longer be checking out your hairdo, they will look where you want them to look—at your handsome face, and more importantly, they will pay attention to what you're saying!"

The young "Your Show Of Shows" comedy writer I mentioned earlier was the first beneficiary of one of my free haircuts. He, too, sported the famous MacArthur comb-over, and after submitting to my tonsorial art and hearing the compliments by Mel Brooks, Sid Caesar, Howard Morris, Imogene Coca and his wife Joan, on his appearance, his confidence was so buoyed that he went on to become the most prolific and successful playwright in the history of the American theater.

Many have referred to Neil as a genius and I concur. Thirty Broadway plays, twenty screenplays and the book for five musicals is what the Reiner-coifed Neil "Doc" Simon created. What else can you call him but genius?

Neil "Doc" Simon

Tom Bergeron And My Old Hot Dog Dilemma

Using a hot dog as a diagnostic tool

CHAPTER TWENTY-ONE

Tom Bergeron And My Old Hot Dog Dilemma

This morning I awoke with a very subtle feeling of nausea and I tested its seriousness by thinking of the two eggs that I had planned to have for breakfast. I lay in bed for many minutes considering the possibility that my eating these sunny-side-up, fried eggs might kill the queasiness. I was most anxious to get my day started, for later that afternoon I had planned to have lunch with my dear old friend, Tom Bergeron.

Tom and I had met a millennium ago in Boston when he was a young, fledgling host of a new afternoon talk show. His show was done 'in-the-round,' which had him skipping up and down the aisles of a circular auditorium where he chatted with and interviewed the 'regular folk' and whatever minor or major 'celebrity folk' the producer was able to collar. I was one of those collared and happy to be so, as I was on tour, hawking my first book, "Enter Laughing." By then, I had been interviewed and had some lively discussions with the seasoned hosts of established shows in New York and Philadelphia. I was surprised and impressed by the assurance and charm with which Tom handled himself. I was impressed by some of the questions he asked about my book, and so impressed that after the show, I told him that he was equal to and in some ways better than others in the field. I remember urging him to think about spreading his wings and plying his craft on a network show in New York or California.

I am pleased that he heeded my advice, but no less pleased than the audiences who have been entertained by his hosting of "Breakfast Time," "Hollywood Squares," "America's Funniest Home Videos" and "Dancing With The Stars."

While pondering my decision to ignore my queasiness and keep my lunch date with Tom, I flashed back eighty-four years to our Bronx apartment at 665 East 179th Street. I saw myself lying in bed and being in the same quandary. I was queasy, it was seven A.M. and I would be late for school if I did not hop out of bed, get dressed and eat my breakfast. Was I indeed too sick to go to school? I did then what I plan to do today, ask myself the following question: *If someone came into my room and offered me, my favorite treat, a hot dog with mustard and sauerkraut, could I eat it?* If I could, I would get out of bed and proceed to school. If I had to refuse it, I would know I was really sick and would remain in bed.

Using that as a litmus test, I had Bess, my secretary, call Tom Bergeron and tell him why I had to cancel our lunch. She did, and scheduled it for a couple of weeks hence—at which time I am definitely going to suggest that we dine any place with a menu that serves great hot dogs.

Tom Bergeron 2012

I Just Re-Remembered Laramie Lois

CHAPTER TWENTY-TWO

I Just Re-Remembered Laramie Lois

In rummaging through a closet that I have not rummaged through in decades, I found the brown suede, five-by-eight-inch writing tablet I carried in my duffle bag during my Army stint in World War Two. Stuffed in its pocket I found letters from Estelle, my newly wed wife, and V-mails from my brother Charlie, who wrote from the war zone in Germany. Also in the brown suede writing tablet was a poem I had written and sent to a young woman I had met at an Army base in Laramie, Wyoming, and before Estelle and I had become a committed couple. I dedicated this lovely poem to Lois. Ever since I wrote about Lois in "I Remember Me" I have desperately been trying to remember her last name. At that juncture, the actual poem I had written to Lois had disappeared and I remembered only its title, "Ode To The Buttocks Bountiful."

The poem was written on two folded, three-by-five sheets of lined paper. They are now yellowed with age and as dry and fragile as the Dead Sea Scrolls.

On the following page is a photocopy of the original Ode to Lois that I wrote seventy-one years ago. On the following page is a legible version that I recently typed.

"Ode to the Buttocks Bountiful"

In any anthology of poetry, carefully bound,

Poems of love and hate, undoubtably could be found.

And wherever one deemed to look or to gaze,

Up would pop Keats with nightingale and vase.

But ne'er has there been in verse or in rhyme,

An ode or sonnet to a curvaceous behind.

To the laws of poets I will not abide,

But write, as I will of the broad backside.

To me this subject is quite as dear,

As love and intrigue was to Will Shakespeare.

So to hell with convention and the great bard,

I'll write as I will of the heinie, firm and hard.

I do not extol, of course, any blase ass,

But of one that belongs to a lovely sweet lass.

A tush that is soft, rigid and white,

Not one flabby, fleshy or slight.

So to you dear Lois, I'deed must ordain,

You are the Queen of the aforesaid terrain.

– PFC Carl Reiner 1942

ballad, rhyme, verse
refrain

Ode to a Buttocks Beautiful †

Anthologie of Poetry
carefully bound
... late or late could
undoubtedly be found.

poem of a nightingale

where ever are deemed to
look as
gaze   beauty
upward pas Keats with night-
ngale or vase +
But never has there been in
verse or rhyme
An ode, or sonnet to a mouth
behind.

soft + rigid +

but is flabby, prized
late
Lois, I'deed
ordain
most surely
Certain

Carl Reine

† Ode to a Grecian Urn

Stan Laurel & Oliver Hardy

Oh For The Days Of Yore

CHAPTER TWENTY-THREE

Oh For The Days Of Yore

This morning, for some reason, perhaps inspired by the memory of the poem I had once written, the poetic phrase, "Oh for the days of yore!" was running through my head, and on a continuous loop. It left me while I had my breakfast and was reading the Calendar section of the "Los Angeles Times" but it returned during my morning stroll around the block. While meandering at a leisurely clip, my brain overheard the following exchange that was going on between Oliver Hardy and Stan Laurel:

Ollie
Oh, how I long for the days of yore!

Stan
The days of my what?

Ollie
The days of yore!

Stan
Yeah, the days of your--finish da sentence, Ollie-
you long for the days of my what?

Ollie
No, no! Stanley, I was saying, "Oh for the days of yore!"
The yore to which I referred, is spelled,
Y-O-R-E, and your "your" is spelt Y-O-U-R.

Stan
Everybody spells "your" Y-O-U-R. But I'm curious Ollie,
which of 'my' days were you longin' for?

Ollie

I am not longing for any of YOUR days, Stanley. Have
you never heard the phrase, "Oh for the days of yore?"

Stan

Yes, many times —just now...from you!

Ollie

Stanley, I'm talking about the classic phrase in literature.
"Oh for the days of yore." Have you never seen
those words written?

Stan

In the book I once read. YOUR was spelled Y-O-U-R.

Ollie

Stanley, you're impossible!

Stan
(Thinks)
You're Impossible??? Ollie, how are you spelling that YOUR?

Ollie

"Y-O-U-apostrophe-R-E."

Stan
(Angry)
Apostrophe R-E? Your doesn't have any E in it.
Ollie, I'm not as dumb as I look. Hmph!

THE END.

Ta Ta!

Treat Your Feet Right And Your Toes Will Thank You

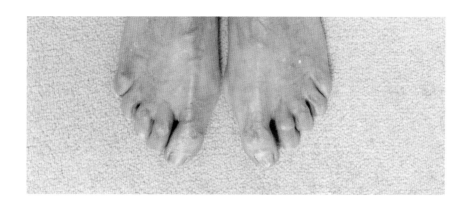

CHAPTER TWENTY-FOUR

Treat Your Feet Right And Your Toes Will Thank You

When I turned forty a great many men my age had found themselves deeply involved in one of the many health regimens that were being offered by reputable doctors, dieticians and physical trainers. The one thing I took most to heart was the need to keep my heart healthy and beating for a long time. To that end, I managed to eat a goodly amount of fresh vegetables, salads, fish, chicken, and eschewed red meats. Six days a week, I ran a mile around the oval track at Beverly Hills High School. After a few years I scaled down the running but kept relatively active by playing weekend tennis with my wife and our friends. I did everything that was recommended, which included buying the very best running shoes extant. Up until this juncture, my feet and toenails were two of my best features. I have always cut my own nails, all twenty of them, and have never had a mani-or pedicure. However, as the years rolled on, I started to develop ingrown toenails--both my big toes and the next-to-pinkie digit on my right foot required professional help. The nails on my big toes were downright ugly. I visited a highly recommended foot doctor who, with surgical precision, and a myriad of cute tools, clipped, snipped, sanded, medicated and neatly bandaged all three toes. I learned from Dr. Zussman (his real name) how and why my pretty nails had turned into ugly ducklings.

He agreed that I had purchased the 'top of the line' running shoes, but then pointed out that I had gotten the wrong size. I insisted that all my life I had always worn shoes that were a ten medium, and he suggested that I should be wearing a ten-and-a-half. It seems that when running, I had damaged my nails by banging them up against the tip of the shoe. It did not occur to me as I had never felt any pain or discomfort.

Subsequently, by purchasing proper fitting shoes, making regularly scheduled visits to the good Dr. Z and his prescribing an anti-fungal solution, 'Formula 3', that I brush on twice a day, the nails on all my toes are looking very much like the ones I owned before I subjected them to hours and hours of close quartered bashing.

A little while ago, as I painted my big toes with the Formula, I thought of something once said of the great silent film star, Rudolph Valentino, who passed away at the age of 31. "Live fast, die young and have a good looking corpse."

I imagined that, when my time came, some crematorium worker might look at me and say to one of his incinerator buddies,

"Hey, get a load of this old guy's feet. His toe nails look eighty years younger than he does. How the heck did he manage that?"

If that funeral worker were lucky enough to have read this chapter he would know that he, too, can have pretty toe nails, if he wears proper sized sneakers and makes regular visits to his podiatrist.

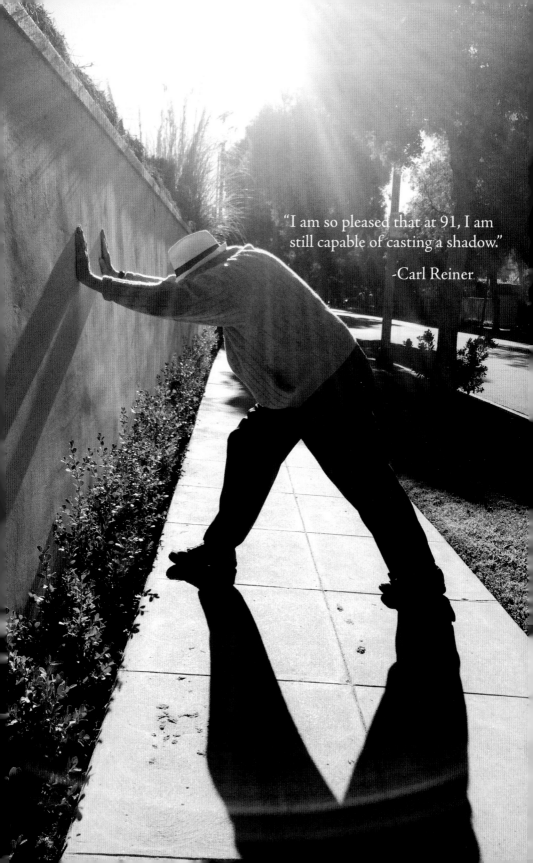

"I am so pleased that at 91, I am still capable of casting a shadow."

-Carl Reiner

DELL

12c

12-230-302

DEC.–FEB.

DR. KILDARE

DR. KILDARE...
DR. KILDARE....
YOU ARE WANTED
IN EMERGENCY

Richard Chamberlain

The Checkups That Allay Checkouts

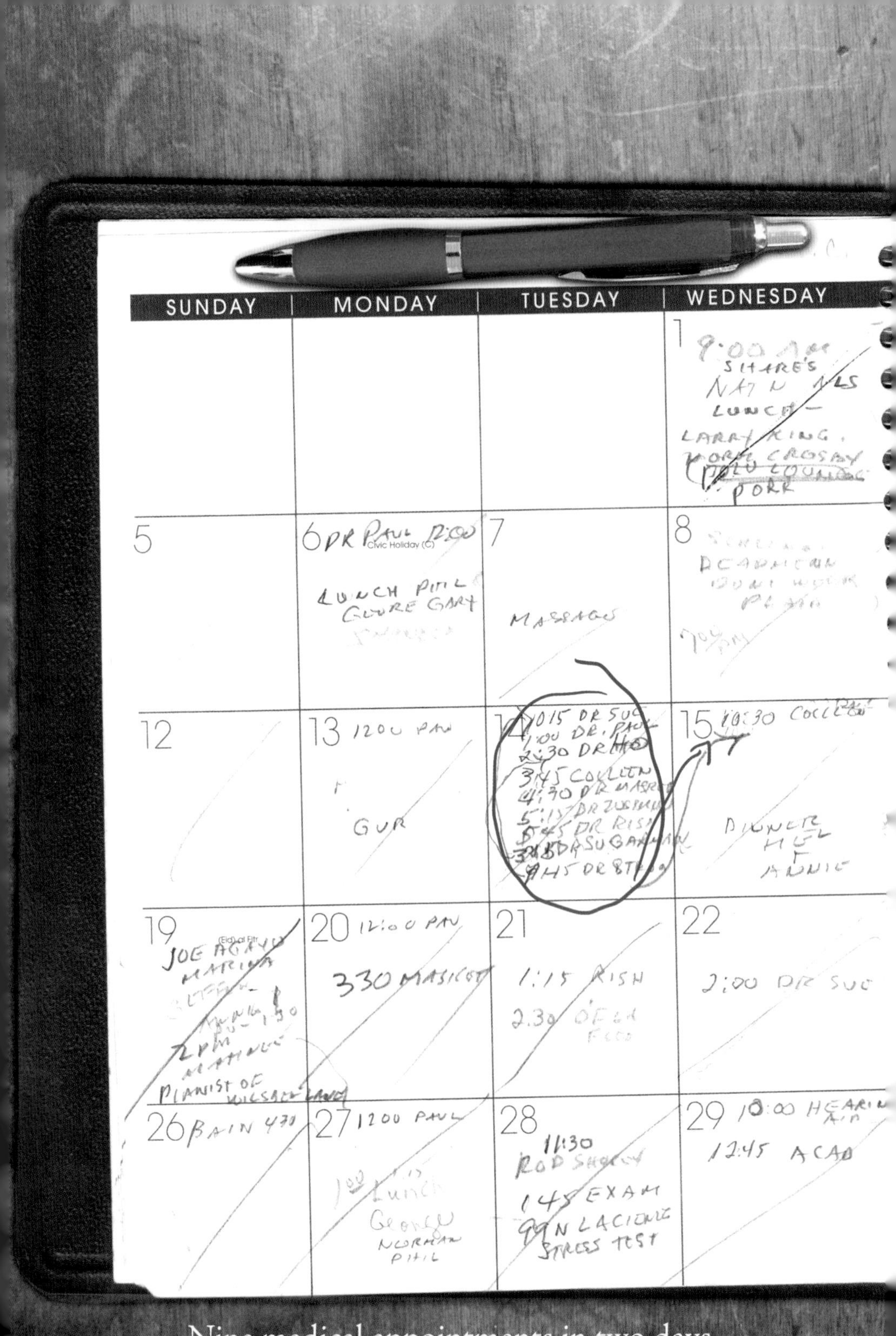

Nine medical appointments in two days.

CHAPTER TWENTY-FIVE

Checkups Can Allay Checkouts

Eleanor Roosevelt, wife of our 32nd President, Franklin Delano Roosevelt, wrote a syndicated newspaper column entitled "My Day," which I considered using as the title for this chapter. I decided against it when I realized that our former First Lady's "My Day" was read by four million readers daily and her column commented on a myriad of diverse subjects. Since my "My Day" covers only one subject, me and what I did today, I felt that my four million readers would agree that "Checkups Can Allay Checkouts" is a more fitting title.

My day started at 8:00 A.M. I awoke and checked my calendar and saw only one entry, a noon appointment with my psychoanalyst. (Yes, once a week, I do see one of those gents, just to find out who I am and how I'm doing.)

The night before, during dinner, I bit down on a hard roll and felt a slight movement in a small bridge that years earlier my dentist had placed between my two lower incisors. It had become dislodged a few weeks earlier on a Saturday afternoon and was reset by a dentist who was covering for my regular dentist. That Saturday, the young dentist noticed a cavity in one of the teeth that supported the bridge and said that he would leave it for my doctor to fill.

I worried about the cavity getting larger and the bridge falling out again, so I contacted my dentist and asked if he could see me today, and he said that he could squeeze me in at 10:15 A.M. I asked if I would be out in time to keep my noon psychiatric appointment and he assured me that I would.

Besides that bridge, all the other teeth in my mouth were ones that I personally grew and they do work well together. What does not work as well as I would like are the muscles in my neck and the bones in my vertebrae. To help improve their functioning, I visit the physical training center I wrote about where, besides hot packs, ultra sound and neck and back massages, I do exercises that help me do all the normal things I need to do, like, walk, sit, stand, lean and improve my posture and balance.

At one o'clock, I called my physical therapist, and asked if it were possible for me to come in today for one of my hourly visits. Two thirty was available and I 'hied' myself to her office, which is but a ten minute ride from my house.

By 3:45 P.M. I was free to continue my historic day-long medical self-improvement drive, and to this end I phoned the Hearing Help Center and asked my provider if she had any time today. My hearing aids were making an annoying whistling sound whenever I upped the volume.

Here, I hesitate to lie and tell you that she told me to come right over but she didn't—she told me she could not see me until 10:30 the following morning. Drat, my historic day of wall-to-wall medical visits had come to an end.

However, as I check my calendar, I see something that may not be as impressive as having seven medical appointments in one twelve hour period, but nine medical visits within the space of a two days is not too shabby an accomplishment. In that two day period, I had scheduled visits to:

1. My dentist: Dr. Strom
2. My psychiatrist: Dr. Paul
3. My physical therapist: Dr. Ho
4. My Hearing Aid Provider: Colleen Moryl, who suggested that a build up of ear wax might be the cause of my whistling hearing aids
5. My eye doctor: Dr. Masket, to have my eye pressure checked for a possible adjustment to the eye drop prescriptions I use
6. My podiatrist: Dr. Zussman, for his professional expertise in helping to make my ingrown toenails become outgrown.
7. My dermatologist: Dr. Rish, for scalp examination and the possible harvesting of benign skin growths before they become non-benign
8. My E.N.T. specialist: Doctor Sugarman, to remove wax from ears (on advice from Colleen)
9. My primary physician: Dr. Sue, for his regular monitoring of blood clotting time as I take prescribed doses of Coumadin

All of this started one morning when I awoke feeling a bit out of sorts. I was not sick but I had no interest in getting out of bed or lunching with a friend. Only two things were on my mind. One was to get to my computer and add the right words to describe worthwhile memories that would make "I Just Remembered" an entertaining and valid, booksized book. The other was to stay healthy so I could do the above. The only way I knew how to stay healthy was to eat plenty of vegetables and fruit and salad and fish, breath fresh air, exercise daily and have regular physical checkups. Which, just twenty minutes ago, I did by visiting Dr. Sugarman, who deftly extracted a half ton of wax from each of my ear canals.

Note: The doctors' names I used are real. However, if they do not wish to be acknowledged and applauded for their dedication, deep knowledge of their specialties and sincere caring of their patients, I may, if they prefer, use fictitious names when promoting this book on TV and the internet. Their call!

Carl Reiner reprises Alan Brady on Paul Reiser's show "Mad About You."

Reiner Receives Record Residual

Carl Reiner directing Sean Young in "Fatal Instinct".

CHAPTER TWENTY-SIX

Reiner Receives Record Residual

Among the many positive things that the Screen Actors Guild, The Director's Guild, The Writers Guild and The Academy of Radio And Television Arts have done for its dues paying members, is the procuring of a proscribed fee for their writing, producing or directing theatrical films or television shows, plus for residual payments should that film or TV show be rerun anywhere.

During my half century as a member of the Guilds, the residuals have been coming in and I will forever be beholden to the aforementioned organizations. I have happily, during that span of time, shown my appreciation by hosting many different Guild functions. The Directors Guild had invited me to emcee their award dinners twenty-five times, which, you must surmise, was because I did a 'good job'... as the guilds have done for me.

DIRECTING   ACTING   WRITING

I have received appreciably healthy amounts of residuals from the projects that paid me well for my initial contribution. Some of those residuals were in the thousands of dollars and each time I see one of these checks listed in the my accountant Al Pivo's weekly statement, I smile and think warmly of all those union organizers who made it happen- these reps who fought hard and long to convince the big studios that the idea of paying artists residuals was not ridiculous but the fair thing to do.

The respect and diligence which now all studio financial officers use to implement the payment of residuals is something I wish now to salute.

Today, Friday, on the 18th of October as I sat at my breakfast table, my assistant Bess Scher handed me the manila envelope that contained the checks I needed to sign that week in order keep our household functioning. After signing the checks, I quickly glanced at the receipts column and saw that there was a check listed in payment for some voice-over work I had done lately for an animated film—and also a dozen or so residual checks in payment for past efforts. One check caught my eye and made me smile. The residual check was for a guest appearance playing Alan Brady on Paul Reiser's show "Mad About You" (for which I received my twelfth Emmy). There were no deductions for agents or managers or fees for government taxes, none! The entire amount of the check was going into my bank account. It was for three cents! Yes, three cents!

SPE CORPORATE SERVICES INC.
800 CORPORATE POINTE
BOX 3636
CULVER CITY, CA 90231

66-156/531 Check Date 09/05/2013

*********************DOLLARS AND 03 CENTS Pay Exactly ******.03

Pay To The Order Of

CLEAR PRODS

VOID 1 YEAR AFTER ISSUE DATE

FOR SERVICES OF CARL REINER ,

MULTI-TONE AREA OF THE DOCUMENT CHANGES COLOR GRADUALLY AND EVENLY FROM DARK TO LIGHT WITH DARKER AREAS BOTH TOP AND B

This has to be a world's record amount for a residual. I was so excited that when Mel Brooks came over that night I told him about my unexpected windfall and he said, "Do you realize that within a relatively short time you could have twenty, forty or fifty cents in hard cash which you can invest in stocks, bonds, real estate or oil wells? Carl-buddy, you are in the cat-bird seat. You can just sit back, and watch that nest egg grow."

None of that had occurred to me, and that is why I feel lucky to have Mel as my buddy. The man knows just about everything about everything.

I will check that statement with Mel. He may want me to edit out the words 'just about.'

A Treasure Trove Of An Elderly Gent's Daily Tweets

carl reiner ✔

@carlreiner

Hollywood, CA · carl-reiner.com

TWEETS	FOLLOWING	FOLLOWERS	
1,537	31	63K	**Following**

  Followed by Robin Williams, Jake Fogelnest, Mindy Kaling and 6 others.

Tweets All / **No replies**

carl reiner @carlreiner · 1h
Mel & I enjoyed watching The Good Wife tonight.. A well written, well acted episode with unexpected twists and surprises.
Expand   ↩ Reply ⇄ Retweet ★ Favorite ··· More

carl reiner @carlreiner · 6h
And I'm happy to read that Mindy Kaling , whom I admire, agrees with my assessment of "Bad Words"
Expand   ↩ Reply ⇄ Retweet ★ Favorite ··· More

carl reiner @carlreiner · 20h
"Bad Words" is a very original and entertaining film with a satisfying comeuppance denouement..
Expand   ↩ Reply ⇄ Retweet ★ Favorite ··· More

carl reiner @carlreiner · Mar 25
Just saw Illustrations by James Bennett for my new young-adult book, "The Secret Treasure Of Kahka Paka " and am noticeably excited?
Expand   ↩ Reply ⇄ Retweet ★ Favorite ··· More

carl reiner @carlreiner · Mar 24
Been told that an 18th century black Cylinder ecording was found with the voice of the 2000 Yr Old Man.. I will believe it when I hear it.
Expand   ↩ Reply ⇄ Retweet ★ Favorite ··· More

carl reiner @carlreiner · Mar 24
Mary Tyler Moore's ten favorite Dick Van Dyke Show episodes available at Target on April First. (and I am smiling).
Expand   ↩ Reply ⇄ Retweet ★ Favorite ··· More

carl reiner @carlreiner · Mar 24
Which most fun for you? Gargling, gurgling, or giggling without gagging? I am guessing the last.

CHAPTER TWENTY-SEVEN

A Treasure Trove Of An Elderly Gent's Daily Tweets

I will now make you privy to what this Elderly Gent does every night before brushing his teeth and going to bed. He spends three to ten minutes typing out tweets that his 52,843 followers might deem worthy and perhaps witty enough to spend time reading. In a little over a year this Elderly Gent has, to date, sent out exactly 1,228 tweets, from which he has culled the ones of which he is most proud, or the least embarrassed to share with you.

He has just brought up the twitter page, and is curious to see how his 1,228th tweet, which he sent out just before he started writing this, was being received.

He reports that his last effort rated 14 'retweets' and 36 'favorites' and he gained 26 new followers. If you are curious as to what The Elderly Gent tweeted, it was:

Mel B and I watched and enjoyed "Rush," Ron Howard directed the film and the wonderful cast brilliantly. Congratulations, Opie.

The Elderly Gent has let me know that he wants to brush his teeth now and get into bed. Tomorrow he will list some of his 1,228 tweets.

It is now one o'clock P.M. Sunday and the Elderly Gent whom, from here on I will refer to as EG, has already fixed himself and eaten an elaborate omelet, which consisted of chunks of lightly sauteed onion, fresh mushrooms, green and red peppers which were tossed into a bowl. He had, with an egg beater, made a fluffy amalgam of the whites of four eggs and the yolk of one, added a dash of soy milk, a splash of cold water, fresh ground pepper and a dash of dill flakes. The EG then poured the egg-coated veggies into a large frying pan in which two tablespoons of Canola oil had been heating. With his spatula, the EG mushed the mixture around until it congealed, then, to complete the dish, he placed the eggs under a pre-heated oven broiler, and kept the pan there until the omelet looked like something he could not wait to consume.

The EG knows he digressed but felt that if his omelet recipe is one you try and like, then the digression will likely bring you more lasting pleasure than any of his old tweets.

Now, to get back to the tweets. The EG has just checked and said that since last night he has added 192 more followers and his group now totals 52, 967.

The EG started tweeting about a year and a half ago and, here now, in no particular order, are some that may be worth your time—or not, I hasten to add, your 'valuable' time, but time when you find yourself without a good book to read or a fair televison show to watch. I just realized that the EG is sounding a little apologetic, and he shouldn't be. I read these tweets and found some of them charming and one or two rather witty. Here are some of his very early ones:

 carl reiner @carlreiner

The photo of me in a cowboy hat was taken when I started tweeting 40 years ago using carrier pigeons.

At times I feel I am having problems with my short term memory. At times I feel I am having problems with my short term memory.

He who speaks with forked tongue should immediately go to the nearest Emergency room.

If ever you are forced to eat crow, skip breakfast.

Ungainliness in the eye of the beholder is ofttimes gainliness to the holder.

Boo the self-serving, absentee congressmen and cheer the self-serving cafeterias who stay open all night.

Don't let anyone bully you, unless they are a licensed bully.

For God's sake I wish people would stop saying for God's sake!

Don't put all your eggs in 1 basket. Less breakage using corrugated containers.

Pity the poor wretch who retches up an expensive meal.

I think Judges who believe in the death sentence should not be referred to as The Honorable but The Intolerable.

A penny earned is nothing to brag about.

Put your money where your mouth is and risk a serious gum infection.

Put your money where your mouth is if you don't mind handling wet cash.

Put your money where you mouth is and get a tenth the interest you would from a bank.

Put your money where your mouth is when a burglar breaks into your home.

Don't let anyone pull the wool over your eyes if you prefer nylon.

I know that "no means no" and "maybe means maybe" but I am not sure what "I am not sure" means".

The words letters and lettuce sound alike but their taste is soooooooo different.

Wearing contact lenses will lessen your chances of dating a Gargoyle.

You cannot buy friendship for less than a hundred dollars.

A 'Know-it-all' rarely knows more than 40% of 'it-all'...if that much.

Examine all options and option any courtroom dramas written by David E. Kelley.

T'is better to have loved and lost than to have hated and found.

Walk a mile in a man's shoes before making him an offer to buy them.

Never sing for your supper before you taste it.

No hero sandwich is a hero to other hero sandwiches made in the same deli.

Some people just don't get it while others get it but just don't want it.

Teach a man to fish and he'll never go hungry! Teach a man to shoot and he'll never need to fish.

Of the following which is edible? Rage, page, stage, cage, pressure gauge of green gage pear? If you said rage, you were waaaay off.

A comedy writer once wrote: "You're more likely to get a laugh if the last word in your punch line ends in a K.* (*Parkyakarkus writer-comedian 1940s Eddie Cantor Radio Show, 1940's)

There is good news and bad news but no good Gnus love bad Gnus.

Felons may be less likely to commit crimes if our prisons served worse food.

Their daughter was condemned to a lifetime of ridicule when Mr and Mrs Forth named their daughter Sally.

An ecstatic hundred year old Pete who used to go "tweet tweet tweet on his piccolo", can now go "tweet, tweet tweet on his computer".

If you can't talk softly, then carrying a big stick will only make you look silly.

In the year 1922 The Ottoman Empire breathed its last breath & Carl Reiner breathed his first.

(On being asked by the Academy to tweet during the last Oscar telecast, our elderly gent, after hearing the list of the recently departed, commented):

I cannot tell you how excited I am to not hear my name mentioned during the memoriam.

(That tweet got a record amount of hits and a lot of laughter.)

Those who exhort the poor to "Make do with what you have!" while they hoard all the stuff with which to "make do", should be arrested.

Do not break doctor, dental or dinner appointments, or wind, or a person's heart, but do brake for Railway and animal crossings.

For the best comeuppance film, rent "The Count of Monte Christo" with Robert Donat and see three very evil men get their just desserts.

Put up: A jar of pickles, Xmas lights, or a pot of coffee, but for an elected, public official, who serves only himself, put up your dukes.

Went to 4 separate yard sales last week and not one owner would sell me their yard.

When young Danny was ridiculed because of his name, his dad Sam Dirtbags legally changed his name to Sam Schitsacks.

Last night I dreamed that I was having a dream only to awake and find out that it was only a dream.

Freud once said about a cigar being a phallic symbol: "Sometimes a good cigar is just a good cigar, but it will never cause mouth cancer."

In the previous tweet I have knowingly misquoted Freud and for this I should have my head examined.

I firmly believe that having gun control, bladder control, climate control and a TV remote control should satisfy most men's basic needs.

Did you ever notice that people who say, "Did you ever notice..." oft times have you noticing something that is not worth noticing.

Praise a good day at night and praise a good Knight for killing dragons, day or night.

A labor of love will always produce something superior to a labor of like.

Rene Descartes said, "I think therefore I am", and I say "I tweet therefore I am" because some tweeting requires some thinking.

To guarantee a long life, get plenty of sleep, eat lots of fruits and vegetables and, exercise daily for at least ninety years.

Those who pinch pennies rarely get time to pinch cheeks or bottoms.

Some grammarians suggest that the musical group, "The Who" should call themselves, "The Whom".

Time and tide wait for no man but tide often lingers for girls who go skinny-dipping.

A fertile mind that can find nothing to tweet about is something to tweet about.

They say: "If, at first, you don't succeed then try, try again". And I say: "... try, try, try, try again". The 3rd or 4th try might be the one that nails it!

Laugh and the world laughs with you, fart and the world laughs at you.

An apple a day will not keep the doctor away if you are married to him.

At ninety-one I am happy to say that I still have all my marbles but sad that I forgot where I put them.

Laughter is not the best medicine if you die laughing.

Inspired by Ms Brown's "Good Night Moon", I wrote "Good Night Loon, Prune, Buffoon, Lagoon, Monsoon, Saloon, Platoon, June & Vidal Sassoon".

Who is more secure than those who can pick their nose in public.

When you dream the impossible dream the odds of fulfilment are much lower than if you had dreamed the possible dream.

Health experts say a hot shower before breakast is much healthier for you than no shower and no breakfast.

"Daddy, what's a tephalone?" "Shhh, it's telephone sweetie, and it was a device people used before they passed the law banning conversation."

Everything worth saying has been said except for: Expleletash, dimosonslaxen, pooquesalt and forbundium.

You are blessed if you have the following three funds: Fundamental, Fundaphysical and Fundaspiritual.

Sales of Pop Tarts are higher than Mom Tarts, Son Tarts and Sister Tarts but still the most popular are a Tart's Tarts.

Some erectile dysfunction can be attributed to earlier erectile functions.

When someone says, "Say no more", oft times they are asking you to say the words, 'no' and 'more'.

If you enjoy a good cry, you may be interested in the handkerchief display on a folding card table in front of Macy's-they're on sale.

Writing about my wife in "I Just Remembered", I have just created a new acronym: LOML which stands for "Love Of My Life".

OBITUARIES

FRÉDÉRIC BACK, 1924 - 2013

Animator's shor[t]
tackled political[...]

BY JESSICA GELT

Frédéric Back, who won two Oscars for his poignant animated short films, died Tuesday morning at home in Montreal, said his daughter Suzel Back-Drapeau. He was 89 and had cancer.

A beloved figure in the world of animation, Back was nominated for four Oscars over the course of his career. He was also a prolific artist and illustrator, getting his start in the graphics department of Radio-Canada's first-ever television station.

Back made his first animation short, "Abracadabra," in 1970. Over the next decade he directed five more shorts before making "Tout Rien," which was nominated for an Oscar for best animated short in 1981.

The film didn't win, but a year later his short, "Crac," got the award. The inventive film, with stylized, painterly animation, looked at the industrial ization of Montreal over decades from the point of view of a simple rocking chair.

After that film's success, he was able to do more ambitious projects and in 1988 won a second Oscar for "L'homme qui Plantait des Arbres" ("The Man Who Planted Trees"). It was about a shepherd's quest to plant a barren valley, and was the first of his films to use speaking roles to further the plot.

Topics such as human disregard for the natural world and the havoc caused by pollution dominated his work. His Oscar-nominated 1993 short, "Le Fleuve aux Grandes Eaux" ("The Mighty River"), was about the impact of pollution on the St. Lawrence River.

"My films have become clichés, studied in universities and animation schools for their technical and cultural content," Back wrote in the detailed autobiography on his personal website. "That goes beyond any-

Back was nor[...]
that politica[...]

thing I might have ho[...]
comforted me, it [...]
employed art [...]
worldwide. [...]

Back was bor[...]
Arbsaß, in a [...]
is now part of Germ[...]
the head of a [...]
mother in Fran[...]
at The Schol [...]
France, where [...]
drawing as a young m[...]

As a child [...]
was drawn and [...]
who took him [...]
same a teacher [...]
rights to the [...]

The natura [...]

Back was nor[...]

SCIENTIST

Janet Rowley's studies in genetics led to significantly better ways to diagnose and treat cancers.

[JA]NET ROWLEY, 1925 - 2013

Researcher
linked cancer
[t]o genetics

BY [...] DISTER

[...]here [...] Janet Rowley was re[...] [...]copted into the [...] University of [...]cal school in [...] for [...]ed [...] Three in [...]

[...]s a [...] [...] for [...]

tified but had, in fact, swapped material with another chromosome. It was that rearrangement that led to a deadly chain of events ending in chronic myeloid leukemia, an uncommon disease that affects about 5,000 people annually in the United States.

It was the first time cancer had been linked to such a chromosomal rearrange-ment, [...]

The Ten Telltale Signs Of
My Encroaching Expiration Date

CHAPTER TWENTY-EIGHT

The Ten Telltale Signs Of
My Encroaching Expiration Date

When, at breakfast, a man reaches for his newspaper and scans the obit page before he does the front page, he knows he is approaching that age. Often I have lamely joked,

"Every morning I check to see if my name is in the obits, if it's not, I have breakfast."

I read the obituary section first, then the entertainment section, then the sports and lastly, the front page. Some days the obits include famous people or someone I knew or had met. I am most interested in their age and am always heartened to read about men and women who have lived past the age I am now. The other day, I happily noted that a gentleman had reached one-hundred-seven, and that he was cheerful and active until a few days before he checked out. I also wondered if the caramel popcorn, on which I was munching, could have a negative effect on when I check out.

If you will indulge me, when I wrote the words, 'checked out,' my mind went to an old friend and collaborator, Aaron Ruben, who co-wrote and co-produced "The Comic," a film I directed that starred Dick Van Dyke. Aaron came up with the phrase that a bystander uttered while watching a film star's hearse being loaded into a van. He and another bystander had this thoughtful conversation:

"Who checked out?"

"Billy Bright."

"Billy Bright?? I thought he was dead."

The phrase "I thought he was dead" often pops into my head when listed in the obits is the name of a little known character actor. I assume that any actor who has not been seen for years has probably 'shuffled off.' I am not sure why, but I am always happy to read that these actors had wives, children, grandchildren, siblings, nieces and nephews and that they enjoyed life before they 'checked out.'

So I'm thinking, '*When will it be my time to go? How will I go? Where will I be when I 'check out?' In bed? At the bottom of the stairway I had just tumbled down? Sitting in my club chair watching Jeopardy? In the shower, bending over to fetch the bar of soap that slipped from my fingers? Driving to Whole Foods to buy artichokes, Dungeness crabs and corn on the cob?*'

Not many days go by without my thinking of my final 'ta ta' or discussing it with friends, family, doctors, close acquaintances or any interested strangers.

My friend, nephew-in-law and manager, George Shapiro, has offered me a deal. He had heard me say that I would love to hang around until I am ninety-four, which was the age my beloved wife left us. George, Estelle's loving nephew, said that if I guarantee that I will hang on till I am ninety-four, he would give me yearly options up to ninety-nine and then throw me a big birthday bash-- after that I "would be on my own."

We have signed no papers, nor will we, as each party trusts that the other will honor the terms of their agreement—for as long as it is physically feasible.

Physical feasability is presently what I have been weighing and I started to jot down some worrisome signs of my encroaching vulnerability:

-After swallowing a prescribed pill, I worry that I have already taken one.

-Trying to remember the name of a film I have just seen and loved.

-Remembering the title, making note of it and then mislaying the note.

-Personally praising Emma Thompson's performance in a film while trying to remember film's title ("Saving Mr. Banks").

-Being greeted excitedly by someone who looks vaguely familiar and refers to the great times we had but gives no clue as to who they are or where it was we met.

-Going to the bathroom at 7:00AM and finding that the hot and cold water taps have been running since midnight—when I last washed my hands.

-The frequency with which I find myself entering a room to get 'something' and stopping short when I cannot remember what that 'something is.'

-Walking toward my car and just before I get to it, I remember why I went into that room —to get my car keys.

-Having to check my calendar more than once to ascertain exactly what day of the week it is and what appointments I have, if any.

-Attempting to memorize the lyrics of an old Irish song, "That Tumble Down Shack In Athlone" (which I have treated in Chapter Eighteen).

It is now 7:00 p.m, the following day and from the time I awoke this morning at nine until three-thirty in the afternoon, I have been battling a queasiness that I attribute to my having overeaten last night. As I lie here working on this current chapter, "Signs of Encroaching Expiration Date," I think, *Prolonged queasiness most certainly fits the bill.*

While waiting for the nausea to abate, I attempt to hasten its exit by drinking a glass of water containing sodium bicarbonate and powdered Zegarid. It works well enough to allow me to go think about writing this book, which, I am told by Larry O'Flahavan, is due at the printer in eight to twelve weeks.

So, apropos of why I may soon be "leavin' y'all," I have, on a bedside pad, jotted down a few more of MY indicators:

-Decreasing mobility

-Decreased virility

-Increasing anxiety

-Disinterest in reading "Variety"

-Quickness to criticize

-Patience to empathize

-Having been issued a handicapped parking placard

209

-Inability to digest food I have loved all of my adult life
-Growing disinterest in taping shows I once looked forward to viewing
-Preferring to watch Dodger games on TV rather than at the stadium
- Not Traveling for more than 30 minutes to see a play, a film or have lunch
-Never having greeted anyone by exchanging a high-five fist bump
-Physical therapy appointment taking precedent over all fun things
-Not accepting invitations to events that include a cocktail hour, a formal dinner, an award ceremony and an after dinner party, even if it is for a star I know, admire and of whom I am very fond, like Steve Martin. I rest my case!*

* Not for eternity—just for now.

"When I could eat whenever and whatever I wanted."

My Papa, Irving Reiner, visits the set of "Enter Laughing" my directorial debut

I Thank You Papa For The Good Advice
And The Good Genes

Carl Reiner & Charlie Reiner 1941

Charlie (10), Irving & Carl (6), 1928

CHAPTER TWENTY-NINE

I Thank You Papa For The Good Advice And The Good Genes

If you are one of the fortunate, who bought, read and enjoyed my bio, "I Remember Me," published in 2013, then you know that my father, Irving Reiner, was a watchmaker and also an inventor. One of his patented inventions was a mantle clock that ran for two years on two AAA batteries. My father also patented a dry-pile battery that powered our pendulum-driven mantle clock, which had worked for sixty years. He had also invented a self-timing shutter for a camera, but some inventor in Japan had patented a similar devise six months earlier.

If you have not read my earlier bio, then you would probably not know that my father was five foot, three-and-a-half inches tall and, when I asked from whence came the height of my six foot brother Charlie, and my six foot one-and-three quarters, he answered, "From my father, your grandfather, Simon Reiner. He was five feet six!"

What I did not cover in that chapter about my father was his wise advice to me when he saw me physically struggling with a problem and mumbling G-rated curse words.

"Carl," he said, "if you want to solve a problem, stop struggling with it. Just relax, look at it calmly-- the solution will be looking right at you."

I cannot tell you how may times those words pop into my head when I find myself wrestling with some physical problem.

I will start with the last time, which was at the soiree given after the screening of "Saving Mr. Banks" a wonderful film that starred the even 'wonderfuller' Emma Thompson. At the party, which was being held at the Beverly Hills Hotel, we were served a culinarily excellent dessert that, for me to fully enjoy, required my recalling my father's advice.

The dessert was served in a small, fluted wine glass that contained two layers, the top layer being an inch of some whip-creamy mixture and, at the bottom, a half-inch of dark, chocolatey pudding. I brought four small flutes and four teaspoons to a table where the lovely actress, Victoria Tennant, her husband, Kirk Stambler, and Larry O' Flahavan were seated. With our teaspoons, we dug out and enjoyed the small amount of custard-like mixture sitting atop the flutes, but all of us were frustrated in our attempts to scoop out the more alluring chocolatey pudding with a spoon too big to reach the flute's tapered bottom.

It was at this moment, I heard my father's voice, "Carl, just relax, look at it calmly and the answer will be looking right at you."

I quickly scanned the table and I saw the answer "looking right at me"—the handle of my spoon!! It was tapered and half the size of the scooping end. I deftly wrapped a paper napkin on the spoon's bowl, and using its handle, I retrieved the once inaccessible, chocolatey treasure—as did all my table companions, who, without instruction, successfully copycatted me.

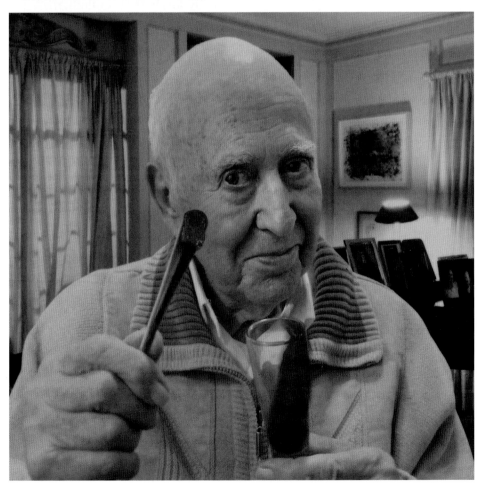

One other time, I was having some difficulty attempting to hang a small, framed photo on a wall. The photo was to hang on the frame's little metal ring. A small nail was needed to accommodate the small ring. My photo was replacing a larger, heavier framed picture that had required a larger nail—which left me with a problem. The head of the nail already in the wall was too big to fit into the tiny metal ring, but when I removed that big nail, it left a hole so large that the small nail disappeared when placed there. It was clear to me that I would have to plug the hole with Plastic Wood, which I did not have, nor had I the time to go out and buy some.

I heard my Pop's voice telling me: "Relax, look at it calmly, the answer is looking at you."—and it was, in the form of a question. "Have I anything I can use in place of Plastic Wood?" and I answered before I finished asking, "Yes, it's in your pocket!" I reached into my pocket, retrieved my package of Stim-U-Dents, snapped three or four of them in half and, with a small hammer, tamped my elegant 'tooth picks' into the hole, and voila, a wood-filled hole that welcomed the small nail on which the frame's metal ring could hang.

Those were but two of the dozens of examples of my father's voice inspiring and informing many of the things I attempted to do—and did!

"Uh, one more thing," to channel detective Columbo again, another memory of my father was jogged as I saw a can of silver polish sitting on a shelf in our broom closet.

I was about eight or nine when my father, to save the cost of paying a professional re-silvering company to replate our tarnished silver-plated eating utensils, found a way to do it at home. Ever the experimenter, by applying some watery chemical liquid to a few dozen copper pennies, he turned them into silver pennies. Until this morning, I wondered what the watery compound was, and by Googling "liquid chemical that silver plates copper." I learned that my Pa used something called Sodium Zincate. My brother Charlie and I were never privy to his experiments, and if ever we asked what it was that he was working on, he would toss his project into a drawer, shut it and explain: "Sieg nisht a naar ahlb arbeit," the German adage, which loosely translated meant, "Don't show people half-work."

Pop let us have some of the silver pennies and bid us not to try to use them as dimes. We did have fun showing our Pop's handiwork to our friends.

To illustrate this eighty-three-year-old tale, I did not use Sodium Zincate, but have painted these pennies with silver paint. That is my personal ninety-one-year-old hand doing the job.

Here I am channeling Papa, silver plating copper

Art Fleming

Why Mel B. and I Knew the Answer to The 1st Question On "Jeopardy"

(Formally "Julann And Her Ten Cent Green Nose Jobs")

Mel Brooks & I discussing with Alex Trebek the big question about "Jeopardy".

CHAPTER THIRTY

Why Mel B. And I Knew The Answer to The 1st Question On "Jeopardy"

A day or so ago when I first thought of writing this story, a four word Mantra-like question was running through my head, "Where do I start? Where do I start? Where do I Start?" Today, serendipity stepped up and handed me the answer. My good fortune came in the form of an email. In it, my manager wondered if Mel Brooks and I would interested in being guest questioners on the show "Jeopardy." Both Mel and I, being committed viewers of the nightly television program, were happy to say "We are absolutely interested!" I cannot tell you how many meals Mel and I have shared as we watched Alex Trebek enter stage left, acknowledge the applause, say, "Thank you Johnny" to announcer Johnny Gilbert and introduce the contestants. Mel and I have another reason for having a longtime personal interest in the show, and the personal interest is because we know and love the person who was deeply involved in the creation of this iconic show, Julann Griffin, nee Julann Wright.

However, before we get to Jeopardy's genesis, I would like to make you privy to one incident in the early life of Julann Wright. I learned about it one Sunday as we sat watching four of our mutual friends playing a spirited game of tennis on her court. Every Sunday, for I do not remember how many years, Julann was the gracious hostess who, besides tennis, offered and served delicious, personally prepared lunches.

Julann Wright was born and bred in the midwest and from a very early age had an interest in show business, and to find if show business had any interest in her she started out for New York.

Using most of her savings for bus fare, she managed to get to Pennsylvania where, to earn enough money to complete her voyage, she bought a few packages of hot dogs and; at a county fair, opened a jerry-built hot dog stand, which turned out to be a bad investment. However, undaunted, Julann hit upon an idea that would help her survive. Taking fifteen cents from the last of her savings, she went to a local Woolworth and bought a small bottle of green paint and a small brush. She went back to her hot dog stand and on its wall, posted a sign: HAVE YOUR NOSE PAINTED GREEN FOR TEN CENTS. I have no idea why anyone would think that this was a viable enterprise, but it was. Dozens of young applicants lined up and had Julann paint their noses green. Julann said that some parents took their green-nosed children to restrooms and washed the paint off, and that a surprising number of the nose-washed kids returned and paid for a second application. Thanks to the tots, Julann made enough money green-painting noses to buy herself a train ticket to New York.

This was the Julann Griffin who now makes her home in West Virginia and who once resided in California, off Mulholand Drive, atop a hill that overlooked San Fernando Valley. It might seem like an exaggeration to say that the Julann of Mulholand Drive was the best hostess in the western world, which includes Washington's District of Columbia's famed Perle Mesta, the "Hostess with the Mostest!" Madame Mesta's popularity was so great that it inspired Irving Berlin to write the Broadway hit musical, "Call Me Madame," which starred Ethel Merman as Perle Mesta.

Perle Mesta's guests were mainly senators, congressmen, and big-wigged Capitol diplomats , but Julann's were film and television actors, and none were big-wigged, just one small-wigged actor, me. I daresay that Perle Mesta's gatherings could not have been anywhere near as much fun as Julann's. Mesta's bunch could not produce in twenty-four hours, the laughter that Mel Brooks alone produced in twenty-four minutes. True, he did have some help from the likes of Gene Wilder, Alan Alda, Gilda Radner, Dick Van Patten, Anne Bancroft, my spouse Estelle, myself and Julann herself.

I decided that to write about the genesis of "Jeopardy," the most popular TV game show of all time, who better than Julann to fill in the details of its conception and birth?

I called Julann, who lives in Virginia in a lovely house on, would you believe, Hellsbend Road? All who know her would expect that Heavensbend Lane is where she ought abide.

Julann and I spoke, and I told her what I was up to and, post haste, by a 'hasteing post' department, I received the following missive:

Hi, Carl,

     I decided to write you tonight in case I get sidetracked tomorrow. I loved hearing from you, and I have to tell you how honored I am that you want to write a thing about me. First of all, you were right...I painted noses green for a dime.

     Early on in our marriage, Merv and I were coming back from a visit to my parents in Ironwood, Michigan. On the plane he took out paper and pen and started to scratch musical clefs and notes, etc. I asked him what he was doing and he said he was trying to think of a new game show. I told him I get so tired of the shows where all the contestants do tricks and jump up and down and do pantomimes, etc. Why can't you come up with an intelligent game with difficult questions and answers. He said that since "The 64 Thousand Dollar" game scandal, you couldn't do it. The producers were caught giving the answers, so they suspected anyone doing a show like that. I said, 'well then why don't you do a show where you give the answers and admit it, and make the contestants come up with the questions?' He said, ' like what?' I said, 'the answer is 5,280.' He said, 'the question is how many feet are there in a mile? I said the answer is, 52 Wistful Vista.' He said, 'the question is, what is the address of Fibber McGee and Molly?' I said, 'the answer is, Cathy Fiscus.' He said, 'the question is, what is the name of the little girl that fell in the well in the 1940s?'

     We kept going like this, and Merv got very excited. By the time we landed in NY we had a game show. Of course, there was plenty of other work to do, but I cooked dinner for all the kid's at the office while they came to the house and had run-thrus, and went to the Salvation Army and bought second hand office furniture to paint and put in a new office for the show. Merv took the show to NBC and they liked it but said it was too hard, so they dumbed it down a little and then it sold. (It was made more difficult after it was up for a while). I once had the temerity to ask Merv why my name wasn't in the credits. He said I couldn't be, because I wasn't a member of the Writers Guild. He said I couldn't take credit because he produced it, and all I did was have the idea. I asked him what idea he would've done if I hadn't given him this one. (No answer)

     And we had our divorce settlement before he sold the game to Coca Cola for 250 million. But if I had reaped any of the rewards I wouldn't be having the fun I'm having now, creating games for the internet.

We expect to have our first app out by the end of the year or the beginning of 2014. The first game is called 'Move Your Vowels.' And I've got about 20 more in the files waiting to be programmed.

I'm glad you feel better, Carl. I think you're doing just great. I watched Bill Maher Friday nite and Chris Matthews was so good. When the Republican guy said we don't know what'll happen if the debt ceiling isn't raised, Chris said, yeah, we don't know what it's like to die either, but do you wanna do it to find out? Good, huh?

Love and XXXXX's, Julann

Son Tony, Grandson Donovan, Julann, Granddaughter Farah, Daughter-in-law Tricia

So there you have it, Julann, an injured party, whose spirit and creativity quickly healed all her injuries. I cannot wait to find out Julann's instructions for her new show, "Move Your Vowels."

By the way, curiosity brought me to Google "Jeopardy," where I read many articles in major newspapers, written by reputable journalists, and all concur that Julann's account of how "Jeopardy" came into being was accurate.

I am so looking forward to this coming Monday when Mel and I are to appear on our favorite game show. We have an ongoing competition when watching it. Mel contends that when we blurt out our questions to the answers, he has been correct more times than I and, reluctantly, I have to agree.*

*Since Mel is a welcome guest in this book, as he is in my home, I can do nothing but agree. However, if and when he writes his bio, he will probably admit that I correctly answer more Jeopardy questions than he does—or at least as many. I'll settle for 'almost' as many.

Julann Griffin

Our Wedding Day, Dec. 24th 1943

Measuring The True Length Of
A Modern Marriage

25th Wedding Anniversary, Dec. 24th 1968

CHAPTER THIRTY-ONE

Measuring The True Length Of A Modern Marriage

My brain smiles when an idea pops into it and it smiles more broadly when that idea has in it the possibility of being expanded to a chapter long enough or interesting enough to include in this book. I am happier still if that idea has in it something that pertains to my wife, Estelle. Such an idea popped when, during an interview, a reporter asked me how long I had been married and I answered, "sixty five years!"

I thought, 'If my wife had not passed away five years ago, I would have said, "December twenty-fourth it will have been seventy years, and while mulling that, my brain smiled as I thought, 'Seventy Is The New Sixty-Five.'

It was strange but I could not let go of the phrase "Seventy Is The New Sixty Five," and for the rest of the day those six words ricocheted on a continuous loop in my head and continued when I lay me down to sleep. While plumping my pillows, I thought of the interview and being asked how long my wife and I were married and having answered "sixty-five years."

Earlier that day, like most days when driving to the market or the hardware store, I got to 'visit' with my wife, by listening to her sweet voice singing some of the 75 great, classic jazz songs she recorded just the two years before passing.

Every night of my life, since her passing, after watching the news or a rerun of "Columbo" or one of the talk shows, I turn off the set, fluff my pillow, close my eyes and whisper, "Good night Estelle, sleep well!" I recently evaluated my answer to the reporter's query about the length of my marriage. I thought about Estelle and me being married for sixty-five years before her passing. Then I thought of myself still being here and nearing ninety-two, and what I would answer if ever again I am asked, "How long were you married?"

"Seventy years and I am still married to her!" Would be my answer!" That night before turning off the lights, I scribbled on my note pad:

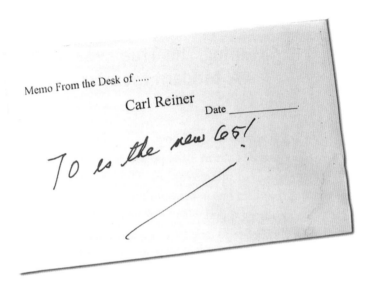

Memo From the Desk of .....

Carl Reiner   Date _____.

70 is the new 65!

Once again I must address those among you who read my last literary effort, "I Remember Me," published early in 2013. In it you may recall the well-written Chapter 22, where I described in loving detail when and where Estelle and I met. That chapter also included my being nine years younger than Estelle, our days apart during World War II, plus the myriad of romantic twists and turns our relationship took before we committed ourselves to one another. If you have forgotten the details, you can refresh your memory by picking up your bedside copy or, if it's not there, asking your friend to return it-- or you can just order a replacement from Amazon.com. I may seem to be tooting my own horn, but "70 Is The New 65!" may very well be a phrase that catches on. Of course, there will be variations, dependent on how long one has been a widower or a widow, so it may be that "60 Is The New 44" or "39 Is The New 32" or, sadly, "12 Is The New 7."

I must say that I feel lucky, nay privileged and somewhat humbled, to have been responsible for coming up with the creation of a new-age adjustable adage:

"70 Is The New 65"

One Must Be 100% Alive to Write About Death

CHAPTER THIRTY-TWO
(THE VERY LAST ONE, MAYBE)
One Must Be 100% Alive to Write About Death

When I awoke this morning and remembered what I had planned for the last chapter of this book, I realized that it would only be possible to write it if I were alive, not dead, and since I am, as of now, not dead, I am able to recall and note some of the things I have done, enjoyed doing and, no doubt, will never do again. They are, for the most part, the simple but important things that most of us take for granted, such as:

Breathing-eating, sleeping-peeing, bathing-washing, writing-reading, thinking-drinking, walking-talking, kissing-cooking, kicking-licking, loving-laughing, lounging-scrounging, speaking-snoring, singing-sighing, coming-going, catching-throwing, mooning-moaning, hosting-toasting, texting-tweeting, giving-taking, selling-buying, burping-farting, hugging-shrugging, strolling-trolling, fishing-wishing, yawning-spawning, skating-dating, mating-hating, meditating-masturbating, voting-doting, nodding-prodding, meeting-parting, hearing-seeing, typing-hyping-skyping, tweaking-seeking, trick-or-treating or just plain being!

There are perks, however, that one gains from being dead. I have listed one perk which you will never again have to worry about:

1. Losing your TV remote control.

Peter Falk

Chapter, The Very Last One After The One Purporting To Be The Last One

or

Once Again I Invoke Columbo's "Uh, Just One More Thing"

Jane Kean (April 10, 1923 – November 26, 2013)

CHAPTER THIRTY-THREE

The Very Last One After The One Purporting To Be The Last One

Once Again I Invoke Columbo's "Uh,...

...just one more thing..." In the preceding chapter I dealt with the problem of being incapable to write about life after one is dead and I thought I had made my last observation on that subject, but today at breakfast I found that I have 'just one more thing' to add. The 'thing' I hope is a salient or at least an entertaining thought about the aftermath of death and or dying. It came to me this morning at the breakfast table, while reading my newspaper. As is my daily wont, the first thing I check are the obits and I think, "If I'm not listed here, I'll have a cup of coffee!" Well, this day I was saddened to learn that someone I had known, the actress-singer Jane Kean had passed away at the age of ninety. She and I co-starred on Broadway in the post-war, hit musical review, "Call Me Mister." We worked together for just a few months but after the show closed, our paths never again crossed. There was a lot to read in Jane's obituary, as she had a full life. I had forgotten that she was on Jackie Gleason's show "The Honeymooners" and played Trixe to Art Carney's Ed Norton. I learned how many times she had married (twice) and to whom, and how many children and stepchildren she raised.

It was the following day that I thought about Jane Kean's obituary and its length. It was at least a third of a page, maybe a half. And then, conceited ass that I am, I wondered, after I have "shuffled off my mortal coil," how long an obituary I will get. How many words will the writer use to inform the world who I was and what I had done with my personal and theatrical life? How many photos will they use, to remind or instruct readers, what I look like now and how I looked when I was younger, handsomer and more agile? And, just now as I was thinking of some classic photos of myself dancing wildly, these conceited, self aggrandizing images I was inner-voicing, suddenly stopped!

Replacing them was a memory of an evening in 2011, "The Academy of Televison of Arts and Sciences" had invited some of my peers, but mostly my 'betters,' to honor me...and they did, to within an inch of my life.

At the end of the evening I was beyond honored, I was downright embarrassed!

After the 'smoke blowing' was over and I was on my way home, I thought, "I am one of the few but lucky human beings who am alive to hear all the positive things that friends and family say before your ashes-filled urn is handed to some relative who thinks, "What do I do with this?"

...uh, just one more thing... I just realized that at my real memorial service (I imagine someone will arrange one), at this one, nicer things will probably be said about me, or if not nicer then with more feeling...

Over and Out

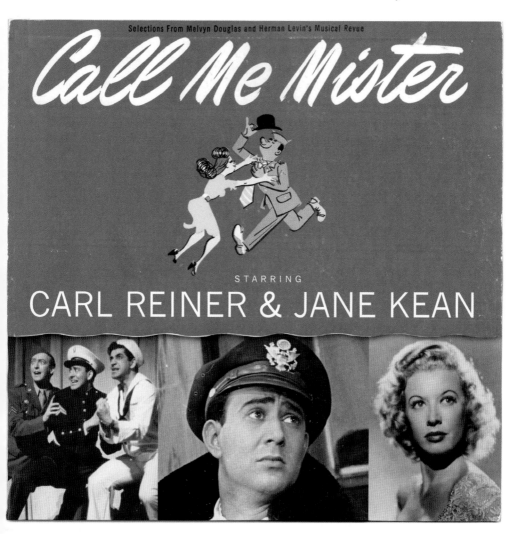

Carl Reiner at his computer adding Chapter 34.

Instead Of Starting An Extremely Short New Bio,
I'm Going To My Computer To Add A Chapter:
Chapter 34

Instead Of Starting An Extremely Short New Bio, I Have Added This 34th Chapter

I am well aware that two pages back I wrote "Over and Out" but, with your kind indulgence, I will amend Falk's Columbo's "Uh, just one more thing" with:

"I pinky swear that it will be my last "Uh, just one more thing for at least eternity..."

Last night, after feeling queasy for too long, I managed to rid my gurgling gullet of some bad things I ingested for dinner. I slept fitfully but managed to dream creatively and humorously, I thought, about nausea and throwing up. I awoke and realized that I had not dreamed anything humorous or useable.

However, a couple of hours later, I had decided that I was well enough to get out of bed and attempt to have a small breakfast, a most original, small breakfast.*

I was about to put on the white shirt I had worn the prior night and discovered that it had a long, long rip in one sleeve- a jagged tear that could not be mended. I was just about to toss it into the wastebasket when my mind flashed back to a pink tin that was once used by the Almond Roca company for its popular Almond Roca Bars.

For years, my wife Estelle, before discarding worn, unusable clothing, would remove all their buttons. Into that pink Almond Roca tin would go an assortment of them snipped from pants, jackets, coats, shirts, blouses and dresses. She had learned hoarding buttons from her Mom, Minnie, who I believe kept her recycled buttons in an old Chase and Sandborn coffee can.

My wife transported her pink Almond Roca button tin from our original Bronx apartment to our first home on Bonnie Meadow Road in New Rochelle, New York,and there it remained in a hall closet until we moved it west to a hall closet on North Rodeo Drive in Beverly Hills, California. The tin and its myriad of buttons I will one day pass on to one of my three children. I have as yet not thought about which of my heirs will inherit the button-filled tin, for as you see, I am still making good use of this seventy-year-old treasure.

* My original small breakfast consisted of eight sliced, hard-boiled QUAIL EGGS on thin slices of whole wheat bread.

Hard-boiled chicken egg slicer, circa 1950

Hard-boiled quail eggs on whole wheat toast, circa 2014.
Thank you Arlene Brown & Salvicion Maglanoc
for your culinary assistance.

Oooh, I Just Remembered What I Almost Forgot

or

Chapter: The Very Last One After The One Purporting To Be The Last One

"When fortisan primpt the falls of famitol I doth whipsnay santimbras forth and all"

-Gumlet, Act 7, Scene 26

CHAPTER THIRTY-FIVE

Oooh, I Just Remembered What I Almost Forgot
or
Chapter: The Very Last One After The One Purporting To Be The Last One

What better closing chapter to a book titled "I Just Remembered" than something, honest to Betsy, I just remembered! Once again, my morning stroll helped to circulate blood to that section of my brain where memories are stored. I found there my unproduced play that I mentioned in chapter eighteen, intriguingly titled, "Shakespeare Misspoke, The Play Is Not The Thing, The Audience Is The Thing!"

I feel strongly that this timeless play I wrote three years ago, can be a crowd pleaser and a profitable venture. However, my mounting or directing a production of "Shakespeare Misspoke..." is unlikely now that I am approaching 'le 92ieme anniversaire de ma naissance' (my tossing in a few French words I learned in the Army adds class to this oeuvre, n'est ce pas?).

I feel strongly that my play's chances of being produced and enjoyed by theater audiences the world over would be served, were I to include a copy of it in this book. So with no further ado, I give you my play to read and the right to obtain the rights to produce: "Shakespeare Misspoke, The Play Is Not The Thing, The Audience Is The Thing!"

Enjoy!

Shakespeare Misspoke, "The Play Is Not The Thing, The Audience Is The Thing!"

A COMEDY IN ONE ACT

By Carl Reiner

PRICE, $1.25

CAST

SAMMMY . . . . *HIMSELF*

MORTON KAYE . . . . *HIMSELF*

SHIRLEY KAYE . . . . *HERSELF*

GRETCHEN FROMME . . . . *HERSELF*

DON LOCASTO . . . . *HIMSELF*

BROOKS HARRISON . . . . *HIMSELF*

ZELDA FITZER . . . . *HERSELF*

GINGER ROGERS . . . . *HERSELF*

ASTAIRE ROGERS . . . . *HIMSELF*

GAYLORD . . . . }

LESSLEE . . . . } *THEMSELVES*

KANTE KANTU . . . . *HIMSELF*

WALT BIGGERLY . . . . *HIMSELF*

JESUS DELGADO . . . . *HIMSELF*

STAGE MANAGER . . . . *HIMSELF*

Scene I, Act I

The curtain parts and, on a raked stage we find a a small, off-Broadway theater. There are about fifty non-matching seats and benches sparsely inhabited by patrons of the art. Some are filled by mannequins appropriately dressed like off-Broadway theatergoers. Making his way down the center aisle is the usher, SAMMY, who is escorting a middle-aged couple (SHIRLEY and MORTON KAYE) to their seats in the third row.

SAMMY

Yours are the second and third seats in. (offers them a single sheet of paper) Here's a program. You'll have to share it. The real ones we don't get until the opening tomorrow.

SAMMY

Exits.MORTON stares at the paper program, grunts, then yawns loudly.

SHIRLEY

(as she sits) Morton, don't start up.

MORTON

What did I do?

SHIRLEY

You grunted and yawned. I don't need you grunting and yawning at me.

MORTON

I wasn't yawning at you, I was yawning because I got only three hours sleep last night.

SHIRLEY

Whose fault is that?

MORTON

Mine! I take full responsibility for agreeing to buy that stupid bed!

SHIRLEY

Again with the bed! You were the one who said we need a new bed.

MORTON

A new bed, not a flotation device!

SHIRLEY

A water bed takes getting used to and when you do, you'll thank me instead of grunting at me.

MORTON

I wasn't grunting at you. I was grunting at this! (taps the program) Look at the title of this play, "Shakespeare Got it Wrong. An interactive Pantomime in Four Acts With Subtitled Dialogue." What is that!?

SHIRLEY

Something experimental-- it could be interesting.

MORTON

Your stomach just growled. You're not going to faint again, are you?

SHIRLEY

I am not going to faint.

MORTON

Well, I might. Why didn't we stop for a bite before coming here? Aren't you hungry?

SHIRLEY

I'd rather be hungry than logy. I cant enjoy a show on a full stomach.

MORTON

And I cant enjoy a show I have no stomach for...

SHIRLEY

Morton, you shouldn't have come! I begged you to stay home.

MORTON

Shirley, our only child is making her acting debut-- how can you ask me to stay home?

SHIRLEY

Laura didn't want you here, either!

MORTON

I don't believe that, Shirley. Why would Laura want me to miss her debut?

SHIRLEY

(embarrassed) Because, in the first act, she has to do a love scene. She said she'd be embarrassed if she knew you were watching.

MORTON

That makes no sense. In high school, I saw her play Juliet. She wasn't embarrassed when I watched her making love with Romeo.

SHIRLEY

In this play Juliet doesn't make love with Romeo, she makes love to another Juliet.

MORTON

You're telling me that our daughter makes love with a lesbian?

SHIRLEY

No, Laura is the lesbian. She seduces a neighbor's straight, teen-aged daughter. You want to see that?

MORTON

(ponders it, sighs) Well, it is certainly not my cup of tea, but I can handle it.

SHIRLEY

Can you also handle that Laura and this teenager are making love on a couch--

MORTON

(unsure) --Yeah, I, I can handle a couch --

SHIRLEY

--and that they're stark naked? That you can also handle?

MORTON

(considers it, then sighs) Well, yes I can, if you warn me before they get naked. I'll just close my eyes and listen to the dialogue.

SHIRLEY

They don't get naked. They are naked when the curtain goes up!

MORTON

(winces, shrugs) So, as soon as I hear the curtain go up, I'll shut my eyes. (nervously checks his watch) Look Shirley, do I have time to take a leak before this thing starts?

SHIRLEY

You're not going to take a leak --you're going out to buy cigarettes!

MORTON

No! But now that you put it in my head, I might. I need a cigarette!

SHIRLEY

Like you needed cancer? Morton, you want to lose another piece of lung?

MORTON

No! And I don't want to see my daughter act like a naked lesbian.
(he starts out)

SHIRLEY

So go home!

MORTON exits and the spotlight picks up SAMMY, leading DON LOCASTO and GRETCHEN FROMME to their seats in the first row. DON is forty-five, sports a worn, characterless fedora on his head and a perky twenty-five year old girlfriend/assistant, on his arm.

SAMMY

Take those two, in the middle. (he gives Don a program) You'll have to share your program with the lady.

GRETCHEN

He doesn't need a program. This is Don Locasto! He's the author of this play. (kisses his cheek)

SAMMY

(suspiciously, to Don) You can't be the author!

DON

(humoring him) Oh? And why can't I be?

SAMMY

Because tomorrow is opening night, and if you was the author, you'd be sitting in the last row. Look, I'm an usher and in every theater I ever ushed in, the authors never sat up front.

GRETCHEN

(butting in) But those authors were not also the director like Mr. Locasto is, and they didn't also have a putz like Sean Luckman for a leading man! Tell him, Honey!

DON

You just told him.

GRETCHEN

(to Sammy) This Luckman guy has never been on a stage before. He knows his lines pretty good, but he never knows when to move and where to stand.

SAMMY

So what's Mr. Locasto gonna do, yell out where he should stand?

GRETCHEN

No, he'll whisper and conduct him, like a band leader.

SAMMY

The people around him are gonna be annoyed.

GRETCHEN

They won't even notice. Mr. Locasto will talk softly..

SAMMY

Even so, they're gonna get pissed. Last year, when I ushed at the Broadloom Theater--

DON

(grabs SAMMY by his shirtfront) Hey, dick-head, it's "when I ushered at the Broadloom theater" not "when I "ushed at"--

SAMMY

(choking sounds) I know that, but by saying "ushed" people remember me. You'll never forget the usher who said "I ushed at." By the way, my name is--

DON

(shouts) -- is gonna be mud, if you don't ush yourself out of here-- now! (releases Sammy, who darts off)

All the AUDIENCE MEMBERS have turned to see from whence the yelling came.

GRETCHEN

(admonishingly) Don, that was not very nice!

DON
(over emoting) I have no time for 'nice'! (takes a dog-eared play from pocket) Do you know the pressure I am under?

GRETCHEN
I know!

DON
You couldn't possibly know! If my play-- (slaps the play's cover and shouts) --does not get the performance it deserves, I could end up in the shit house without a flusher. (stands up, announces too loudly) I am getting the hell out of here!

The AUDIENCE reacts and a spotlight hits MORTON and SHIRLEY.

MORTON
(stands up) Lets go, Shirley! That was the playwright, and even he doesn't want to be here!

GRETCHEN
(laughing) Sit down folks, Mr. Locasto is not going anywhere. He was just saying some lines from the play, and he said one of them wrong.

AUDIENCE happily chats about being in on a theatrical gaffe.

DON
Which line did I say wrong?

GRETCHEN
(takes his script from him, opens it) Guess.

DON
Damn, did I say shit house again instead of crapper?

GRETCHEN

(humoring him)Yes, Mr. Locasto, you said shit house instead of crapper--

DON

Maybe I should change it to shit house.

GRETCHEN

No, crapper is classier and, in most of the previews, Sean Luckman said it right.

DON

He did. Now, if he can only manage to deliver the pizza to our naked lesbians without getting a boner, we may be in business.

Light on SHIRLEY and MORTON, who stands up to go.

MORTON

 I am out of here!

SHIRLEY

Sit down, Morton. Don't you want to see an actor get a boner on stage?

MORTON

I do not and neither should you! Or did you forget that it's your naked daughter who inspires his erection.

Light irises out on MORTON and SHIRLEY and come up on the opposite aisle where SAMMY is escorting a very heavy set couple, JOAN and JOHN ARBUCKLE. Each is carrying a huge bag of potato chips. SAMMY points to two wooden kitchen chairs located in the center of the forth row.

SAMMY

I'm sorry, but those bags make too much noise, they won't let you eat during the show.

JOAN

(clutching her bag of chips) We're not. We're going to finish these chips before the show starts.

JOHN

My wife and I are in the show. We understudy the roles of Ginger and Astaire Rogers, the morbidly obese theatergoers.

SAMMY

Are you pulling my dingle?

JOHN

No, we're not! (with a self-satisfied grin) Check the program.

SAMMY

(reads from program) Ginger and Astaire Rogers: morbidly obese theatergoers. Millicent and Monroe Larson

JOHN

We understudy the Larsons-- (points to spot in program) See. Joan and John Arbuckle.

JOAN

John's great-great-great grand uncle was Fatty Arbuckle. He was a big star in the silent movies!

SAMMY

Never heard of him.

JOAN

Well, the director heard of him, and that's why he hired us. He didn't think we were morbidly obese enough, but Fatty Arbuckle was and we convinced Mr. Locasto that it's in our genes to gain weight fast.

JOHN

We started gaining weight just two weeks ago, and we are having a ball!
We drive in and out of "In 'n Out Burger" four times a day. When
they see us drive up, they have four jumbo, extra fatty, triple bacon
cheeseburgers and two orders of fried onion rings packed and ready
to roll.

JOAN

Honestly, this job is a dream, come true. (pops a chip in her mouth)

The spotlight irises out on JOAN and JOHN and picks up SAMMY
leading a handsome, middleaged man, wearing a once-elegant tuxedo.
He is the theater critic, BROOKS HARRISON. Aiding him is his
blonde, adoring, younger companion, ZELDA FITZER.

SAMMY

Row three, seats one and two. (offers program) You'll have to share
this. It's the preview program.

BROOKS

(gingerly holds program between his thumb and forefinger, speaks with
an English accent) How quaint! Paper programs for preview nights! It
does not inspire confidence in their undertaking. However, the word
'undertaking' does inspire an opening line for my review. (takes out
pad and taps pocket) Damn, I forgot my damn pen! Zelda, do you
have a pen?

ZELDA

There's one in the glove compartment. Shall I go get it?

BROOKS

Don't bother. (stands and addresses the audience) Folks, may I have
your attention?

The AUDIENCE turns toward the speaker.

BROOKS

Hello! I am Brooks Harrison, the senior theater critic for the "Staten Island Weekly Digest" and unless I can borrow a pen from one of you kind folks, I will be unable to critique the offering we see tonight. Is there a volunteer?

THE AUDIENCE is amused and all seem willing to oblige. GRETCHEN and SHIRLEY come down the aisle to BROOKS and simultaneously offer their pens.

SHIRLEY

Here Mr. Harrison, you can use mine! Its a uni-ball gel Impact. It never skips.

GRETCHEN

(hands hers to him) But in case it does, you can use my Bic as a back up!

BROOKS

(tests both on his pad) Thank you, Ladies. I will use both your pens, alternately, to review this preview performance of "SHAKESPEARE WAS WRONG. THE AUDIENCE, NOT THE PLAY, IS THE THING!" I sincerely hope that what we see on stage tonight does not make us want to throw up!

Spotlight goes out on BROOKS and GRETCHEN, and up on, GAYLORD and LESSLEE, two very handsome, young men who follow SAMMY down the aisle to seats adjacent to DON LOCASTO and GRETCHEN.

SAMMY

Your seats are those two next to that guy with the hat. He's the director.

GAYLORD

We know who he is! (moves to his seat, then cheerily) Hi, Mr. Locasto. We are here!

LESSLEE

And may I add, very excited to be working with you.

DON

Oh, yes, you're the guys I hired over the phone to do special makeup.

LESSLEE

And some choreography, if needed--

DON

Yes, if needed. Tell me your names again.

GAYLORD

I am Gaylord.

LESLEE

And I am Lesslee.

DON

Are you saying Leslie?

LESLEE

No, Lesslee, double S, double E.

DON

Oh, yes the Cutler brothers, Cutler, not with a C, I think you said. How do you spell it, with a K?

GAYLORD

No, with a Q--Q-U.

DON

Really, you spell Cutler, Q-U-T-L-E-R?

LESLEE

(spells) Not E-R, A-H! Q-U-T-L-A-H.

GAYLORD

Do you love it?

DON

It's pretty freaky.

GAYLORD

(Stiffens)By freaky, you mean gay, don't you?

DON

(good humored) Well, it is a rather campy way of spelling Cutler, wouldn't you say?

LESSLEE

(upset, barks) No, Mr. Locasto, we would not say-- campy!

DON

Easy now. Why are you getting so upset? I was just curious about why you changed the spelling?

LESSLEE

(suddenly angry) Why? I'll tell you why! Mr. Locasto. Because spelling Cutler, Q-U-T-L-A-H, looks and sounds less Jewish than C-U-T-L-E-R, which is our real name!

GAYLORD

We were born Leon and Garry Cutler and we are Jewish, and all of our lives, we took such shit from anti-Semites and gay bashers like you that we decided to change one of our identities--

LESSLEE

-- and the easiest one to change was the spelling of our Jewish name, OKAY?

DON

(smiles warmly and salutes) I love it. Welcome aboard, brothers.

271

GAYLORD

Brothers? Don Locasto?

LESLEE

You're Jewish and gay?

DON

Close. Scottish and I'm not gay but I love Broadway musicals. My name
is Donald McTavish. A Scot doesn't stand a chance. It's the Scorceses,
the Coppolas, and the De Sicas, who get the all the respect and the
jobs! So I'll be Locasto for awhile. Now, let's get back to why I hired you.

GAYLORD

Primarily to do makeup.

DON

Yes, and on the phone, you mentioned that when you were younger,
you both worked as street mimes.

GAYLORD

In San Francisco. And you want us to do mime makeup for some of the
actors?

DON

Yes, and maybe yourselves.

LESSLEE

You want us to be in the show?

DON

I think that any show would benefit with the addition of two extremely
handsome, talented gay gentlemen! (lightly) You are gay, aren't you?
(they exchange quick looks)

GAYLORD

(playfully) If we are not, we can certainly play gay.

LESSLEE

(going along, cheerfully) It's a stretch, but I know we can adjust.

DON

I'm sure you can. Now watch the show tonight and maybe come up
with some ideas for a--

GAYLORD

--a short ballet of some sort--

LESSLEE

--using a chorus line of dancing street mimes, perhaps?

DON

Perhaps! (GAY and LESS do a giggly high-five, a balletic twirl, and sit.)

Spotlight irises down on LESSLEE and GAYLORD and comes up on
the center aisle. Down it comes a uniformed hospital worker, JESUS
DELGADO, negotiating a small wheelchair in which sits MR. WALT
BIGGERLY, a frail ninety-year-old who depends on a portable oxygen
tank to keep him functioning. He uses a cane to prod people who get in
his way. All of Walt's speeches will be accompanied by much wheezing
and coughing.

WALT

Wheelchair-- coming through! Move your butts. Jesus, park me--
third row!-- for Christ sakes-- set --the damn-- parking-- brake!

JESUS

Si, senor, I set! (parks chair by Brooks)

WALT

(taps BROOKS with cane, wheezes) Brooks Harrison-- Thanks for
coming. Are the seats okay? We held these two wooden ones for you--.
(gestures to Jesus for oxygen mask)

BROOKS

The seats are okay. Who are you?

WALT

(takes off mask, wheezes) Walt Biggerly-- this is my theater-- one of the nine off, off, way off- Broadway theaters--- in the Biggerly chain--- and I'd be grateful if the review you write-- (puts mask back on)

BROOKS

Mr. Biggerly, if you are looking for me to write a good review, you are going about it in the wrong way.

WALT

(takes mask away) Tell me the right way.

BROOKS

There is only one right way. Produce a seriously good play-- or offer me a seriously good bribe.

WALT

How seriously good a bribe are we talking about?

BROOKS

Well, if I were still reviewing for the New York Post, it would be five thou.

WALT

But you don't write for the New York Post ---you write for that Staten Island Weekly rag.

BROOKS

Digest! That's Weekly Digest!

WALT

I'll give you fifty bucks!

BROOKS

Make it a hundred!

274

WALT

Make it fifty!

BROOKS

How about seventy-five?

WALT

How about fifty?

BROOKS

Let's say sixty-five.

WALT

Let's say twenty-five!

BROOKS

Let's say fifty!

WALT

Said!

BROOKS

That is, if you pay me the fifty as soon as I write the review--

WALT

I'll pay you after I read it!

BROOKS

Then I'll get to it immediately. (whips out notebook and pens)

WALT

You are going to write a review of the play before you see it?

BROOKS

It is how I work. I never allow my personal opinions to influence my review. It keeps me honest. Here we go. (recites as he writes)

Last night at the Walt Biggerly Way, Way Off Broadway Theater,
I had the privilege to be one of the ninety-nine audience members
who witnessed the brilliant premiere of "Shakespeare Was Wrong",
a modern masterpiece in four acts by the gifted writer-director, Don
Locasto. For this spectacular, soul-satisfying work of art, Mr. Locasto is
certain to be awarded this year's Pulitzer Prize for outstanding drama!
(hands review to Biggerly) If you had any class, you'd pay me the
hundred for that!

                         WALT
I never had class, and you won't get the fifty-- unless you give me
another paragraph! (wheezes loudly, shouts.) Christ, Jesus-- where's my
oxygen! (Jesus hands Walt the mask.)

                         BROOKS
For fifty bucks, I'll give you a two sentence paragraph.

                         WALT
(wheezes) Four sentences!

                         BROOKS
Three!

                         WALT
(wheezes) Start writing.

                         BROOKS
Stop wheezing!

BROOKS starts writing and WALT, surprisingly, stops wheezing. Iris
out on BROOKS and up on a very tall, very handsome, very dark-
skinned, African American young man, KANTE KANTU. He checks
the ticket in his hand as he approaches the row where SHIRLEY is
seated. MORTON has not yet returned to his seat. Shirley is napping,
and is snoring lightly. KANTE KANTU telescopes his long frame
into a small, metal folding chair as he glances over at SHIRLEY. He
then focuses on his program. Something in it makes him smile. He

notices something on the floor, reaches down to recover a ladies purse.
He looks at SHIRLEY, who is asleep.

KANTE KANTU

(with purse in hand, he whispers) Madame, Madame---

SHIRLEY opens her eyes, sees a big, black man holding her
purse and gasps.

SHIRLEY

(paralyzed with fear, stutters) Wha, wha, what do you want? Tha,
that's my purse --but if you want it - ttake it, ttake it--it's yyours!

KANTE KANTU

I don't want your purse.

SHIRLEY

(on the verge of fainting, crosses her arms) Whaddya want? Mm mee?
Y y you wwant mm mee? No, no, please don't rape me!

KANTE KANTU

(lays the purse atop her folded arms) Whoa, whoa, Madame, calm
down. I am not going to harm you. For the record, I am not a thief or
a rapist. I was invited to come here, as I understand everyone in the
audience was, to see this new, experimental play. By the way, my name
is Kante Kantu.

SHIRLEY

(clutching her purse) Wha, what kind of name is Kantoo Kantoo?

KANTE KANTU

(correcting) It's Kante Kantu and it is an African name.

SHIRLEY

You, you are an African!

KANTE KANTU

(playfully) Is it that obvious?

SHIRLEY

(sputtering) Oh, absolutely. Very obvious! I noticed it immediately,
but I want you to know that I am very open minded. I am not bigoted.
My husband Morton, who should be back any second, has many, many
good friends, and many of those good friends have at least two Negro-
Afro-American friends. Once in a while, they even play ball together.
(stops and changes subject) Do you know anything about this play?

KANTE KANTU

Only that it needed a lot of rewriting. I hear that the only scene that
seems to work was a nude, love scene.

SHIRLEY

(gasps)A nude-- love-- scene? You came all the way from Africa to see
that?

KANTE KANTU

No, but I would have to see this particular scene. My lady friend is one
of the nude actors.

SHIRLEY

(gasps) Your lady friend!?

KANTE KANTU

Yes. She's listed in the program. (refers to it) See? Betty Lee Bankhead.

SHIRLEY

Betty Lee Bankhead--? (sighs relievedly, mumbles) -- thank God,
its the other girl!

KANTE KANTU

Betty Lee Bankhead is her stage name. I prefer her real name, it suits
her better, Laura Kaye.

SHIRLEY

(screams) Laura Kaye? Oy, my daughter goes with a Shvartzah! (grabs her heart and faints)

Iris out on SHIRLEY and in on BROOKS, who is smiling.

BROOKS

(starts scribbling in pad) Ah, would that we hear dialogue in "Shakespeare Was Wrong" as humorously provocative as this. (reads from pad) Oy, my daughter goes with a Shvartzah! Words worthy of a first act curtain line!

End of Act 1, Scene I

Act 1 Scene 2

It is fifteen minutes later and order has been restored. MORTON has returned and SHIRLEY, who is now holding a bag of potato chips, pops a handful into her mouth. ASTAIRE and GINGER ROGERS are hovering. SHIRLEY speaks with her mouth full.

SHIRLEY
(referring to bag of chips) Thith wath tho nithe of you thir -- (swallows, then enunciates clearly) I was trying to say, This was so nice of you, sir, your potato chips were a lifesaver. I don't know why I fainted--

MORTON
You fainted because you haven't eaten for a whole day, and neither have I! (grabs a handful of chips from the bag) Shirley, I thought you were dead. I came back from a smo --a walk, I came back from a walk, and I find you lying in a heap. What the hell happened?

SHIRLEY
I don't know! I must have dozed off and had this horrible nightmare-- I cant remember--

GINGER
(pops chips in mouth and munches) You were mumbling about someone trying to steal your purse and your virginity--.

SHIRLEY
--I don't remember that, thank God-- and thank you for these chips, (pops some chips in her mouth and hands bag to Ginger) --they were a God send.

GINGER
You keep 'em. We have another whole bag. I'm Ginger Rogers. My husband Astaire and I are understudies in the show.

ASTAIRE

We understudy a morbidly obese couple. We're not nearly fat enough yet but we are working on it. (pops potato chips in her mouth)

SHIRLEY

I think you're plenty fat.

ASTAIRE

Not compared to the actors we're understudying, they find it hard to walk.

GINGER

If we keep at it, hopefully, we should soon find it hard to walk!

MORTON

(enumerating) Morbidly obese understudies, naked lesbians on a couch, what the hell kind of play is this?

ASTAIRE

From what we could see at rehearsals, it's basically a pantomime.

SHIRLEY

A pantomime! You mean where the actors don't talk?

ASTAIRE

Oh, they talk. They do pantomime when they're not talking.

GINGER

And sometimes they do pantomime while they're talking. It's very avant garde.

ASTAIRE

By the way, the pantomimists are all professionals. A couple of them studied mime with the great Marcel Marceau's first cousin, Martin...

MORTON

Martin Marceau! I can hardly wait. (reaches for his pack of cigarettes) I'm going for a smo --walk--

SHIRLEY

A smoke! Morton, you've already lost half a lung-- and you say you're going for a smoke?

MORTON

I did not say smoke, I said, smo walk-- a small walk. I'm going out for a small walk. I'll be back in a minute--

MORTON starts out but stops when the lights dim.

SHIRLEY

You don't have a minute. They put a spotlight on the curtain. The play is going to start.

MORTON

Who's that?

A man, wearing a work shirt, steps from off the stage and to the first row of the auditorium.

ASTAIRE

That's our stage manager.

STAGE MGR

Good evening, folks. As you know, this is our the last preview performance before our opening, tomorrow night. First, I would like to welcome you all to our newly refurbished Tiffany Theater.

Audience laughs and hoots.

MORTON

(shouts into his cupped hands) Refurbished from what, a dumpster?

SHIRLEY

(yells) Wait till Tiffanys hears they named a toilet after their store!

STAGE MGR

Good, I see we have a very discerning audience. If you will bear with me, I have a few short announcements that I am obliged to make. First, I'd like to remind you to turn off all cell phones. How many of you are carrying a cell phone?

ALL AUDIENCE MEMBERS raise their hands.

SHIRLEY

(waving both her hands) I have two and I am turning them both off.

STAGE MGR

Madame, you are a good citizen! Now, if everyone follows suit, we can get under way. As soon as you have shut off your phone, raise your hand.

One by one, they all comply.

STAGE MGR

Well done. I thank you.

A musically annoying cell phone goes off and continues to ring.
No one moves.

STAGE MGR

(cupping his ears, asking coyly) Am I the only one who hears a cellphone ringing? C'mon now, whose is it?

BROOKS

(fishing in his pocket) It's mine. Zelda, help me!

STAGE MGR

Will you please shut it off?

ZELDA

I will if I can find it. It's in his jacket lining. Ah, I found it. I'm getting it out, I'm getting it, I'm getting it, I got it!

BROOKS

(grabs for phone) Don't hang up! (whispers into it) Five bucks on Sundown in the third to win--

STAGE MGR

Are you quite finished sir?

BROOKS

No! (into phone) -- and in the sixth, ten across the board on Bad Personality.

STAGE MGR

Sir, if you don't mind, some of us came to see a play.

BROOKS

Then stop talking and let the actors start!

STAGE MGR

Thank you, I will do that! Oh, one last thing. As you know, in unwrapping candy, the cellophane makes a lot of noise, so as not annoy your neighbors when the play is on, please unwrap them now..

All dig pieces of candy from their purses or pockets and start unwrapping. GINGER and ASTAIRE bring forth a bag full of giant lemon drops and wrestle the cellophane off a dozen of the candies. Other audience members work on removing wrappers from Life Savers, Thin Mints, Kit Kats, Tootsie Rolls, Licorice Whips and Abba Zabbas. The STAGE MGR waits patiently throughout the unsheathing.

STAGE MGR

While you are unwrapping and before we ring up the curtain, the management of Tiffany Theater asks that you to join them in helping the less fortunate among us, the community's needy children. Sammy, our usher, and I will be accepting donations. So give whatever you can to a most deserving charity. (walks to first row in his aisle as Sammy does in his) The money you give tonight will go to an organization appropriately named FU FUKED! It stands for Fund For Underwriting Kindergarten Education. FU FUKED, a charity that helps children who have, for too long, been FU SCREWED! For the collection, you notice we are using coffee cans. We do this so you can avoid embarrassment by contributing money that doesn't clink.

The STAGE MGR and SAMMY pass amongst the audience. Spotlights will illuminate those contributing. All but DON, WALT and JESUS will contribute non metallic money.

GAYLORD
(dropping bills in the can) This is from my brother LESSLEE and me. We went to a Kindergarten that was supported by this charity.

LESLEE
Were it not for FFUKED, we would have been.

STAGE MGR
I thank you all for your contribution, and the dedicated FFUKED workers thank you. We are now just moments away from enjoying the premiere performance of "Shakespeare Was Wrong." To assure that there are no distractions, the restroom doors will be locked, and since the first act is rather long, if you feel a need to go, I suggest you go now!

ENTIRE AUDIENCE rises, starts up the aisles.

STAGE MGR
Whoa, whoa, whoa! Hold on! There are only two stalls in the ladies rooms and one stall and a urinal in the mens room, so unless you want to stand in line, let us return to our seats and do this in an organized way. We will start with the front row. When one exits, another enters.

The MEMBERS mutter about the efficacy of the STAGE MGR's instructions. Blackout!

End of Act 1, Scene 2

The theatergoers are all back in their seats and listen attentively to the STAGE MANAGER, who is addressing the audience from a side aisle.

STAGE MGR

I am very proud of you. Of the hundreds of odd audiences I have ever dealt with, you are the least odd!

AUDIENCE laughs.

STAGE MGR

And, you have toileted faster than any of them! (checking his clunky pocket watch) You have accomplished the difficult run in seventeen minutes and six seconds, an all time record! Come on, give yourselves a great big hand!

STAGE MGR is joined by all of the AUDIENCE, including MORTON, who was goaded by SHIRLEY.

STAGE MGR

Congratulations to you all. Now sit back, enjoy and interact with, "Shakespeare Was Wrong!"

Just as the word interact is uttered a cell phone goes off. This time it is not BROOKS HARRISON but an equally grating musical fanfare blares from it. Somebody quickly answers it. All we hear is a male voice whisper angrily, then snap the phone shut.

STAGE MGR

(suddenly, out of control, shouts) Okay, that does it! I trusted that you were all serious theatergoers but I guess I misjudged you. I am really fed up and you have left yourselves, and me, with only two options. Either hold on to your precious cell phones and force us to cancel tonight's performance, or surrender your phones and let us hold them until the show is over. Your choice. You've sixty seconds! Sixty seconds!

KANTE KANTU

(emoting with stentorian voice) I need but six! If you recall, William Shakespeare, The Bard of Avon, wrote "The 'Play' is the thing!" He did not write, "The 'Phone' is the thing." (in his normal voice) I paid to see a play, not hear a phone! Join me, my friends, lay down your phones as a good soldier will lay down his arms when the battle is over!

With a flourish, KANTE hands his cell phone to the STAGE MGR as if surrendering a weapon. Spotlight moves from KANTE to LESSLEE.

LESSLEE

(holding phone aloft) Gaylord and I are good soldiers--

GAYLORD

...and we'd like to join that big, beautiful black man who just laid down his phone!

The two men mimic Kante's surrendering of a weapon. The spotlight then moves to SHIRLEY.

SHIRLEY

Morton, we must see our daughter's acting debut!

MORTON

I know, I know! I must see her, even if I have to keep my eyes closed! (shouts toward STAGE MGR) Hey Mr. Manager, you got our two phones.

SPOTLIGHT moves to ASTAIRE.

ASTAIRE

And you have mine and Ginger's!

GINGER

(shouts out) C'mon everybody, give 'em up!

BROOKS, WALT, DON, GRETCHEN and ZELDA all raise their hands and hand over their phones.

STAGE MANAGER

(ecstatic) Thank you, thank you! We will return your phones as soon as the show is over. Now, we can get on with the--

MORTON

(puts up his hand) Uh, Mr. Manager, just one thing! A lot of the phones are the same model. How do I go about getting my own phone back?

STAGE MANAGER

Simple. You use my phone, punch in your number, then pick up the one that rings.

ALL APPLAUD as the STAGE MANAGER strides to the first row.

STAGE MGR

Thank you! And now, Ladies and Gentleman, in a few short moments these curtains will part and you will experience the last preview performance of Don Locasto's interactive drama in four acts, "Shakespeare Was Wrong." And to help you interact, with the play and the performers in it, you will all be presented with a tube of Max Factor's theatrical greasepaint, which, for close to a century, was the favored makeup of our nation's greatest street mimes. Those of you who apply it to their face, will automatically become eligible to perform as inter-actors. I promise you, it will be an experience you will forever cherish. Now, do we have volunteers?

A great many hands shoot up, including some of the mannequins (whose arms will be manipulated by hidden stage hands).

STAGE MANAGER

Wonderful. Keep you hands raised. Now, to assist you in transforming yourself from the handsome man or pretty woman you are, into a street mime who closely resembles this man-- (unfurls a poster of Marcel

Marceau) Monsieur Marcel Marceau, here are our two professional makeup artists, brothers Lesslee and Gaylord Qutlah!

Spotlight on LESSLEE and GAYLORD, who now sport Marcel Marceau white-faced Mime make-up. The brothers approach MORTON and SHIRLEY.

LESSLEE

A tube of greasepaint for Monsieur! (hands him a tube)

MORTON

What the hell am I supposed to do with this?

SHIRLEY

Morton, weren't you listening? You put it on your face!

GAYLORD

Exactly, but first take the cap off. And one for Madame! (hands her tube)

MORTON

(has opened the tube) This looks and smells like the stuff I put up my ass!

SHIRLEY

Morton, that is not funny.

MORTON

Neither are hemorrhoids. This looks like Desitin Ointment. (explains to Lesslee) That's what I use for my hemorrhoids.

LESSLEE

Well, this is for your face.

GAYLORD

You do know your ass from your---? Call us if you need help.

GAYLORD and LESLIE exit.

MORTON

(laughs) Those guys are funny, but I'm not smearing this gunk on my face.

SHIRLEY

Morton, your daughter is acting in this play! Putting on this greasepaint will show that you support her!

MORTON

Shirley, I can't do this!

SHIRLEY

You have to!

MORTON

No, you have to do this. I don't know how to put on makeup. (squeezes a dollop into her hand) Here, make me look like a schmuck!

Light irises out on MORTON and SHIRLEY and comes up on BROOKS and ZELDA.

ZELDA

Brooks, this is such fun! (kisses her tube) Don't you love it!? Say yes!

BROOKS

If you want me to say yes, ask me if I hate it.

ZELDA

(squeezing out greasepaint) Oh, come on Brooksie, let me make you up! Pleeeaaease, it would so exciting!

BROOKS

I see nothing exciting about looking like a dumb ass dork!!

ZELDA

(purrs seductively) Not even if you looked up at the mirrored ceiling in your bedroom and saw that 'dumb ass dork' lying naked next to this sweet-assed dork giving you a blow job?

BROOKS

(squeezes tube and greasepaint erupts as he quietly sings ala Sinatra) "Start spreading the gooooooo."

ZELDA

(sings to "New York, New York") I'll do it today--I want to be a part of you --You Dork, You Dork!

BROOKS

(sings) Start spreading the news--I want you to stay-- and hang around a heart that is, Your Dork's, Your Dork's.

ZELDA

I want to wake with your head on my titty -- awake not asleep--

Fade out on ZELDA and BROOKS and up on KANTE KANTU's back. He is looking into a mirror that SAMMY is holding.

SAMMY

How much longer are you going to take?

KANTE KANTU

I'm almost there!

SAMMY

Everyone has finished.

KANTE KANTU

Everyone started out white. I had to use three layers of this demeaning glop to cover my blackness. (makes a final dab, turns) Ta Da! How do I look? (he is white-face except for his thick lips which he left 'au naturale')

SAMMY

Like a black-faced Al Jolson wearing white face and your real African lips!

KANTE KANTU

Exactly what I was striving to capture, the face of Mister Bones, a nineteenth century, racist Minstrel!

They laugh and exchange hi-fives.

Iris out on KANTE KANTU and in on the STAGE MANAGER.

STAGE MGR

People, people, may I have your attention? Sammy, can we turn up the lights?

The lights brighten. All have finished their makeup and, for the most part, have been successful.

STAGE MGR

Oh, I wish you could all see what I see, a sea of very credible Marcel Marceau look alikes. Would all of you newly minted mimes please stand up, show yourselves to each other and then give yourselves a great big round of applause?

THE AUDIENCE does as asked. They point, laugh, chatter, then break into applause.

STAGE MGR

I am sure many of you have questions about why, to see tonight's interactive play, you were asked to put on mime faces. Well, I am here now to answer any and all questions.

MORTON

(stands and shouts) I have two questions. One, why the hell did you ask us to put on this fakata makeup? And two, who's idea was it to hire my daughter to play a naked lesbian in your fakakta play?

DON

(jumps up) I'll answer those questions, if it's alright with you, Lou?

292

STAGE MGR

It's more than alright, it's fitting. Ladies and gentleman, the author and director of "Shakespeare Was Wrong," Mr. Don Locasto!

The audience applauds lightly as DON stands.

DON

You are too kind. Sir, before I can answer your questions, tell me what fourcockter means, you used that word, fourcockter, twice.

MORTON

For your information, Mr. Lacastas, it's fakakta, not fourcockter.

DON

(correcting him) And for your information, it's Locasto, not Lascatas, if you don't mind!

MORTON

I don't mind if you don't. And as for fakakta, it's a Yiddish word meaning shitty which, I'm guessing, your play probably is.

DON

(sacastically) Oh, you are guessing my play is shitty!? Have you ever read it?

MORTON

I don't have to, I can tell from your fakakta title. "Shakespeare Misspoke, The Play Is Not The Thing, The Audience Is The Thing." What a cheap trick, using Shakespeare's name in the title to make customers think they're going to see something classy. You're a flimflammer, Mr. Lascastas!

SHIRLEY

(stamps her foot angrily) Stop it Morton, enough already! Go out and smoke a cigarette!

MORTON

Butt out, Shirley! Mr. Lascastas and me--

DON

(screams out) Mr. LASCASTAS and ME?? You dare criticize my writing when you don't have the slightest knowledge of grammar or how to pronounce a man's name. It's not LASCASTAS and ME! It is LOCASTO and I!

MORTON

(screams) Go to hell, Mister whatever your name is! How was my grammar and 'pronounciation'? Good enough for you to get my drift, you sanctimonious schmuck?!

SHIRLEY

(slaps him hard on his arm, screams at the top of her lungs) Enough already, Morton! You're making me crazy, you're making yourself crazy and you'll make everybody craaaaazsseeee--

MORTON

Keep screaming like that and you'll give yourself a heart attack. Will you do me a personal favor and take a deep breath! Please? You want to faint again?

SHIRLEY

(she takes it and calms down) Not particularly. But at least I wouldn't be hearing you call the director a sancta something!

MORTON

(still seething) Schmuck! Sanctimonious!

SHIRLEY

I never heard you use that word--

MORTON

Neither did I. I didn't know I knew that word. I'll bet there are plenty more where that one came from-- that I don't know I know.

SHIRLEY

Morton, do yourself a favor, go home!

MORTON

I'll go, but not until after I see my daughter act.

SHIRLEY

(addressing the audience) With your eyes closed, you are not going to
SEE her act.

MORTON

I know, but I'll HEAR her act, and, okay, after I've heard her, I'm
skedaddling! Look, 'skedaddling,' another new word!

DON

Wonderful! So why don't you start skedaddling now and take your wife
with you!

SHIRLEY

I am not skedaddling anywhere, I paid for these seats.

DON

No you didn't, I compt'd both of you!

MORTON

(shouts to the world) Compt'd, shmompt'd, I'm not leaving until I
hear my daughter act.

DON

Nobody is going to hear anything unless you two shut up! Folks, raise
you hands if you want these two motor mouths to shut up!

No one raises a hand for a long beat, then both MORTON and
SHIRLEY raise theirs.

DON

(shaking his head in disbelief) Only two hands? (addresses Morton
and Shirley) And they belong to you people. I don't get it! Why did you
two raise your hands?

SHIRLEY

I did because I want him to shut up. My head is pounding!

MORTON

And I want her to shut up so they can start the play. I want to hear my daughter act!

DON

(shaking his head) I am confused. Why didn't you folks out there raise your hands?

The sheepish AUDIENCE MEMBERS turn to each other and mumble, some smile, some chatter and some look confused.

BROOKS

Sir, I think I speak for the majority when I suggest that this crude, ill-mated couple have afforded us more entertainment than the scheduled play is likely to. Clap your hands if you agree.

ALL applaud heartily.

BROOKS

I was mistaken, I did not speak for the majority, I spoke for all of you!

SHIRLEY

Not for me. He doesn't speak for me. I came to see a play and I will not say another word until I do.

MORTON

Me neither. Put on the play and, 'I promise 'I will keep my trap shut' are the last words you will hear from me tonight! I promise you that!

AUDIENCE laughs, cheers and applauds.

DON

Thank you Morton, you have just given us a perfect segue to an explanation of why we are here and why I asked you to wear mime faces.

MORTON

(shouts, cupping his face) Oh, I gotta hear this perfect segue. Why did you ask us to wear these fakakta faces.

AUDIENCE laughs.

DON

Morton, what happened to your promise, "I will keep my trap shut are the last words you will hear from me tonight?"

MORTON

I already broke that promise.

DON

When did you do that?

MORTON

When, after saying "I promise that 'I will keep my trap shut' are the last words you will hear from me tonight," I said, "I promise you that," which broke my promise.

AUDIENCE laughs, enjoying the exchange.

DON

(laughs, shakes his head) You're right, you fakata son of a bitch!

MORTON

I take that as a compliment. Now, I'm still curious about why you talked us into sitting here with Desitin ointment on our faces. Folks, aren't you a little curious too?

AUDIENCE voices agreement.

MORTON

Okay, back to your perfect segue, Mr. Locasto!

DON

(pleasantly surprised) Well, thank you for pronouncing Locasto correctly!

MORTON

And thank you for pronouncing 'fakakta' the traditional way.

DON

(laughs) We live and learn!

MORTON

Okay, back to why the mime faces--

DON

Well, I assume that you are all here to hear the words spoken by the actors who perform in "Shakespeare Misspoke, The Play Is Not The Thing, The Audience Is The Thing." Well, to help understand why "The audience is the thing," I would like to call upon our dedicated scholars of the art of Pantomime, Lesslee and Gaylord Qutlah.

LESSLEE and GAYLORD bounce up to a tepid response.

LESSLEE

Thank you, Don. Ladies and Gentlemen. Now, to guarantee optimum enjoyment of this evening's event, we ask for your indulgence. In the next few minutes you will learn of a land and a culture that, sadly, has been ignored and in some cases, all but forgotten--

GAYLORD

--but thanks to Don Locasto's play and the dedication of a handful of oft-times maligned artists, change is imminent. The land my brother spoke of was smaller than Rhode Island but its influence was huge. This fifty-five square mile peninsula was called Pantomimia!

LESSLEE

The citizens of Pantomimia were dubbed Pantomimians and their art came to be known as Pantomime. This soulful but dying medium still exists but there are fewer and fewer artists equipped to do it justice.

GAYLORD

So tonight we invite you to celebrate with us and hopefully join in as practitioners of the great and ancient art of Mime! Those of you who would like to participate need do nothing more than stand up!

AUDIENCE reacts.

KANTE KANTU

(stands up) What are we required to do?

LESSLEE

Nothing, until everyone is standing.

ASTAIRE

(tries to help his wife get out of seat) Up you go, Ginger!

GINGER

(tries and fails) Up I'd like to go! I cant, my foot fell asleep!

ASTAIRE

(continues to struggle) Our getting obese has some drawbacks, like getting up out of a chair. (grunts and curses) Jesus!

JESUS

(who is close by, answers) Yes, I am Jesus. You want I help?

ASTAIRE

Oh, Christ yes!

JESUS

Christ no! Delgado yes! I Jesus Delgado. (evaluates the situation) You want rise Madam?

ASTAIRE

(mocking gently) Yes, Jesus, we want 'rise' Madame.

Working together, JESUS and ASTAIRE, with much grunting and strain, manage to get GINGER on her feet.

GINGER

(ecstatic) Oh, my God Jesus rose me! I feel so biblical!

LESSLEE

(standing in the center aisle) Now that everyone is standing, I would like you to try performing some of our traditional pantomimes. First, let's us do 'walking against the wind.' (shouts toward the stage) Lesslee, turn on the wind machine!

From offstage, a huge blast of wind blows right into the faces of the standing mimes. All flail and shout, and one of the mannequins has his wig blown off.

DON

(waving his hands, shouts) Whoa, whoa, Gaylord, Lesslee--- whoever turned on that damned wind machine, turn it off!

The wind machine stops.

DON

(almost apoplectic) What the fuck are you idiots doing?!

LESSLEE

(snaps angrily) Teaching rank amateurs the art of pantomime, and how dare you call us fucking idiots, you no talent putz!

DON

I did not call you fucking idiots, I said, what the fuck are you idiots doing? And how dare you fucking idiots call me a no talent putz.

GAYLORD

(steps into the auditorium) We dare because we are not fucking idiots but you are a no talent putz who can't see that the wind machine makes a mime's 'walking against the wind' pantomime look one hundred percent more authentic.

LESSLEE

Two hundred percent! For the first time ever, we have just seen a mime's hair and scarf moving as if the wind were actually blowing.

DON

But the wind IS actually blowing!

LESSLEE

No, the wind is not blowing, you putz, it's a big electric fan! Gaylord, keep the fan going. Tell him, folks. Say: "Look, Locasto, it's a big electric fan, it's a big electric fan. Join me folks, "Look, Locasto, it's a big electric fan--"

SHIRLEY, GRETCHEN, ZELDA. SAMMY and JESUS, all in good humor, join in chanting.

LESSLEE, GAYLORD and ALL THE ABOVE

(yell out) Look, Locasto, it's a big electric fan! Look, Locasto, it's a big electric fan! Look, Locasto, it's a big electric fan! Mister Locasto. Look, Locasto it's a--

Suddenly an ear piercing woman's scream is heard. Immediately, the room becomes silent, then:

GRETCHEN

(yells out) Mr. Kaye, Mr. Kaye come quick. Your wife has fainted!

MORTON

Oh, my God, I knew it, I knew it! Damn damn, damn!

GRETCHEN

She can't breath! She's can't breathe!

MORTON

(runs to her, shouts) Shirley, Shirley, hang on. I'll be right there!

The whole AUDIENCE stands and looks to MORTON who is racing to WALT BIGGERLY'S seat where he commandeers the old man's oxygen tank.

MORTON

I need this! (grabs mask off Walt's face and runs) My wife can't breathe.

WALT

(gasping) Neither-- can I--- give me back --my mask--
(calls out) Jesus-- where-- are-- you--?

JESUS

In crapper-- (flying down aisle, zipping up his fly) I hear scream. I come. Where mask? Where tank?

WALT

(gasps and points) He took 'em-- that guy-- Jesus, I-- can't-- breathe-- Jesus-- help me ---
WALT faints into JESUS' arms.

JESUS

Yes, I help-- Jesus help! (carrying Walt, looks heavenward, begs) Jesus Christ, por favor, you, help, Jesus Delgado help, si? (he crosses himself)

DON

(runs to Jesus) Hurry-- follow me!

DON leads JESUS, who is carrying WALT, to where SHIRLEY lies. Lights out on DON and WALT and up on MORTON and GRETCHEN arriving at SHIRLEY'S prostrate body. MORTON sets tank down.

MORTON

(putting mask on Shirley) Alright Shirley, breathe-- you're going to be okay, just breathe in and out-- in and out-- you gonna make it, honey! (looks to Gretchen) She is going to make it isn't she?

GRETCHEN

If she can take a breath, she might, but her lungs aren't working--

DON and JESUS, carrying WALT, arrive. JESUS sets WALT down.

302

WALT

Give me --my mask-- Jesus get my--

MORTON

(snatches mask off Shirley's face) Here, take it!

MORTON gives the mask to JESUS who puts it on WALT'S face.

GRETCHEN

What are you doing!?

MORTON

Shirley can't use it now-- she's not breathing!

BROOKS

(shouts out) Nobody can breathe. The air is stifling in here!

ALL THE AUDIENCE agree, some start fanning themselves.

DON

We can fix that. Lou, turn on the fan-- full blast!

STAGE MGR

You got it!

THE GIANT BLOWER strikes again, blowing clothes and programs about.

MORTON

(shouts) Shut it off, damn it! My wife doesn't need a hurricane, she needs mouth to mouth.

THE FAN shuts off, and with that, MORTON pries open SHIRLEY'S mouth and proceeds to give her mouth to mouth. Almost immediately, she stirs.

SHIRLEY

(in delirium, with her eyes closed, she screams out) NO, NO! I DO
LOVE YOU, KANTE KANTU, BUT I AM MARRIED!

MORTON and the ENTIRE AUDIENCE are stunned, and after an
uncomfortably long silence, they laugh, applaud and deliver a standing
ovation. Only MORTON, SHIRLEY and KANTE KANTU do not
join in.

SHIRLEY

(opens her eyes, sits up, looks about and wonders) Where am I? What's
going on?! Why is everybody standing and applauding and why did
they just stop applauding?

MORTON

They stopped to hear what you were saying.

SHIRLEY

What was I saying?

MORTON

Uh, before or after you opened your eyes...

SHIRLEY

Start with after.

MORTON

Well, you said, "Where am I? What's going on? Why is everybody
standing and applauding and why did they stop applauding?"

SHIRLEY

Now, why would anyone want to hear that?!

MORTON

Because they didn't hear it originally so they couldn't know how
unimportant it was.

If the things I said were unimportant, why where they all standing and applauding?

MORTON

They applauded because you regained consciousness.

SHIRLEY

I was unconscious?

MORTON

Yes, and you came to when I gave you mouth to mouth resuscitation.

SHIRLEY

Ich! That was you?? (shows disgust by spitting and wiping her lips)

MORTON

Who did you think it was?

SHIRLEY

(confused) My husband.

MORTON

I am your husband!

SHIRLEY

You can't be. Kante Kantu is my husband and he is as black as the ace of spades.

KANTE KANTU

(shouts out) Shirley, I am not your husband and I do not appreciate your ultra-racist description of me.

SHIRLEY

And I don't appreciate your putting your long African tongue down my short Jewish throat.

BROOKS

And I do not appreciate what is going on between those amateurs!
(bangs his shoe against his seat) Hey, Locasto, did you not invite us
here to see your new play, or are we here to listen to other invitees
spew repetitive, inane, boringly bad badinage? If it's the latter, you have
succeeded admirably!

DON

Boringly bad badinage? I'm sorry you feel that way. I, for one, was
rather amused by the exchange between Shirley and Kante Kantu.
How say all of you?

GAYLORD/LESSLEE

I found it entertaining! / Yes, and rather erotic!

KANTE KANTU

As did I.

SHIRLEY

Frankly, I never expected I'd enjoy that kind of kiss.

MORTON

Shirley, what the hell has gotten into you-- besides Kante's tongue?

SHIRLEY

I don't know. As a teenager, I thought that french kissing was
disgusting. Some guy soul-kissed me at my sweet sixteen party, and I
threw up all over him.

MORTON

Some guy? That was me!

SHIRLEY

You? I thought it was my cousin, what's his name?

MORTON

Leo! No, you threw up on him at our engagement party. How could you not remember that?

SHIRLEY

Hey, give me a break, I was just unconscious. I'm lucky I can remember who you are. Who are you? (stops, stares at him)

MORTON

(aghast, shouts) Who am I??

SHIRLEY

Oh, calm down! I know you're my husband, but what's your name? Don't tell me, I'll get it. Milton, right?

MORTON

Morton!

SHIRLEY

Close enough!

ASTAIRE

(raises his hand and shouts) Hey, Mr. Locasto, we came to see the play. If we are going to understudy the roles of the Morbidly Obese Couple, we'd like to see what we're in for.

GINGER

To tell you the truth, Don, I hate mimes and I don't know if I want to understudy a mime--

ASTAIRE

--and can we get some water?

WALT

(wheezes) and-- some ox-- y-- gen--

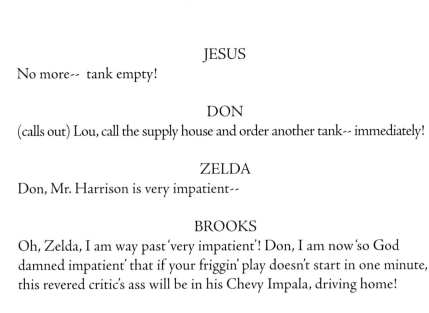

JESUS

No more-- tank empty!

DON

(calls out) Lou, call the supply house and order another tank-- immediately!

ZELDA

Don, Mr. Harrison is very impatient--

BROOKS

Oh, Zelda, I am way past 'very impatient'! Don, I am now 'so God damned impatient' that if your friggin' play doesn't start in one minute, this revered critic's ass will be in his Chevy Impala, driving home!

DON

Which friggin' play are you referring to, Mister Harrison?

BROOKS

Your friggin' play with that friggin' ostentatious title, Mister Locasto! (mockingly) "Shakespeare Misspoke, The Play Is Not The Thing, The Audience Is The Thing." You know I'm beginning to suspect that there is no play.

DON

Oh, there is a play alright and I dare say a very unusual one, one that you will never, ever forget you saw.

BROOKS

And you wrote this unforgettable play?

DON

No, you did!

BROOKS

(laughs) Oh, did I?

DON

Yes, but not alone.

BROOKS

(humoring the nut) Of course not, I have a collaborator, don't I?

DON

Oh, yes indeed.

BROOKS

Well, I would love to meet him.

DON

You will meet them all!

BROOKS

All? Where are these collaborators of mine?

DON

Right out there! (sweeping, open armed gesture) There are your collaborators! Each and everyone here in Walt Biggerly's newly refurbished Tiffany Theater has collaborated on the writing of "Shakespeare Goofed!"

BROOKS

(his mouth drops, and then a huge smile breaks out on his face as he recites) "The Audience, Not The Play, is The Thing!" So, all of us, the people you gave free tickets to, are the actors in this--this real life drama.

DON

Yes!

BROOKS

Unfrigginbelievable! How did you come to this bizarre idea?

DON

I didn't come to it, it came to me. About ten years ago, I went to see this Broadway play and--

A noisy entrance of TWO PARAMEDICS carrying a fresh oxygen tank for the stricken WALT.

DON

I'll continue as soon as the paramedics attend to Mr. Biggerly, who, by the way, seems to be alert.

WALT

(wheezes and coughs) Con-- contin -- ue -- now -- I --have to hear-- why-- I'm a colla--bor--at-- or-- but tell-- it faaass--

JESUS

Fast! He say, tell fast. He not so healthy.

DON

(speaks fast) Okay, I was at this Broadway theater and the play we were watching--

WALT

(wheezes) Lou-- lou-- louder--

JESUS

(shouts) He say louder! No good ears!

DON

(shouting) Okay, okay! This play we were watching was awful. I whispered to my wife, Estelle, that I'd bet that everyone in the audience had a more interesting story to tell than the one the author was telling.

BROOKS

And when you got home, you sat down at your typewriter...

DON

...computer! I didn't get to it until years later. I had forgotten about it, when Sybil, a secretary who worked with me way back then, reminded me of this idea I'd mentioned.

MORTON

Mr. Playwright, can I ask you a stupid question?

DON

I am sure you can.

MORTON

If there's no play, then my daughter, who was supposed to play a naked lesbian, won't be acting tonight?

DON

No, she will not be acting tonight, or any night, if I can help it..

MORTON

Good, thank you! No further questions!

DON

Unless someone has a question--

LESSLEE

We have. Gaylord and I wondered what you have accomplished with your little pastiche.

GAYLORD

Yes, Lesslee and I have worked our little butts off thinking there would be something we could show for our efforts, and poof, it's over and we're left with egg on our faces.

LESSLEE

(touches his face) More like egg whites.

DON

(smiles) That was funny.

LESSLEE

Thank you. It was meant it to be.

ASTAIRE

Ginger and I agree with them. We feel let down.

GINGER

What do we do now? Fold our tents and live off our memories?

DON

Well, you do have that, but if memory fails, you can always watch the video tape.

LESSLEE

The video tape? What video tape? We didn't get any video tape.

GAYLORD

Did anyone get a video tape?

ZELDA

Brooks and I brought our own-- the video tape of Sinatra singing "New York, New York"--

BROOKS

That's an audio tape--

ZELDA

Oh, you're right, that's an audio tape not a video--

MORTON

Audio, video, shmideo-- who gives a shit!

DON

You should give a shit! You all should! I have been shooting this video tape since the moment Sammy ushered you, or should I say 'ushed you' to your seats. By the way, copies of this historic video are available and can be purchased for the low price of forty-nine, ninety-five.

BROOKS

Mr. Locasto, this is outrageous!

DON

I disagree. Forty-nine, ninety-five is a very fair price for a--

BROOKS

Damn it, I was referring to your video taping me without permission!

DON

With or without your permission, Mr. Harrison, our cameras are continuing to record you!

DON nods toward SAMMY, who smiles and waves.

BROOKS

Cameras? More than one camera?

DON

Actually, four. We are using a multi camera technique. One that Jerry Lewis helped to develop.

MORTON

(looking about) I don't see no multi cameras. I don't even see one multi camera. Where are they?

DON

The four cameras are mounted in the proscenium!

MORTON

Oh yeah, and where is this, this 'proscemimum'?

DON

(smiles, shakes his head) Sir, this 'proscemimum,' or proscenium, as some pronounce it, is the structure right in front of you. Hidden behind it are the four video cameras-- each one manned by an operator. Okay gang, pop your heads out and say hello to the stars of our production.

From behind the proscenium, we assume that the four men have popped out and are mirroring what we see the audience doing, waving, laughing and generally enjoying the moment.

DON

"Smile everyone, you're on Candid Cameras!"
The AUDIENCE break out their toothiest smiles.

BROOKS

Hold it!! Before you smile anymore, I think it behooves Mr. Locasto to
tell us what he intends doing with this unauthorized video tape.

DON

You who have smiled have not smiled in vain, for I have arranged a viewing
of our unauthorized video as soon as we can lower the screen and load it
into the projector. I have every confidence that after you see it, and hear the
enthusiastic response it provokes, your authorization will be forthcoming.
(turns toward projection room) How are we doing there, Sammy!

SAMMY

(offstage) Screen in place! Projector loaded! It's all yours, Mr. Locasto!

DON

Okay folks, as your director, I am going to ask you folks to take over!
At the count of three, I want you all to shout out, with conviction, the
magic words, "Roll em!" Here we go, One-- Two-- Three!

AUDIENCE

(at the top of their lungs, yell) ROLLLLL EMMMMM----

The screen goes to black and a second later we see a screen and
projected on it, is the handwritten title:

SHAKESPEARE MISSPOKE
THE PLAY IS NOT THE THING
THE AUDIENCE IS THE THING

The title fades, and we see projected on the screen, the auditorium of the Tiffany Theater just as it was seen at the play's opening. We see Sammy leading Morton and Shirley Kaye down the center aisle to their seats. We see and hear Sammy say, "Yours are the second and third seats in. Here's a program, you'll have to share it. The real ones we get tomorrow for opening night."

The scene continues with Sammy exiting and Morton grunting and yawning. We see and hear Shirley saying, "Morton, don't start up and his answering, "What did I do?"

After this scene, a very, very, very, very slow fade out starts and continues over Morton and Shirley's exchanges.

(Imposed over the above scenes, we also hear the voices of Morton, Shirley and Sammy commenting on what they are watching)

Sammy: "I should have worn my lighter shirt."

Shirley: "Am I that fat-- or is it the camera?"

Morton: My yawning looked very natural-- and also my grunts.

The screen finally continues to fade while Morton is saying, "I wasn't grunting at you I grunted at this, Shakespeare Misspoke, an Interactive Pantomime in Four Acts with Subtitled Dialogue" and when he says, "What is that?" it fades to black!

THE END

Oh, Just One More Photo...

Me and LOML*

*The Love Of My Life

My fifty-year-old father, Irving...

...and his ninety-year-old son, Carl.

More eBooks & iBooks by Carl Reiner
Available on Amazon & iTunes:

All Kinds of Love

Continue Laughing

How Paul Robeson Saved My Life And
Other Mostly Happy Stories

My Anecdotal Life

NNNNN

Just Desserts: A Novellelah

I Remember Me

The Secret Treasure of Kahka Paka

Photo Index

Alley, Kirstie, 146
Allison, June, 3
Amsterdam, Morey, xii
Arthur, Carol, 238
Astaire, Fred, 84
appointment book, 182
audience, 140

Bancroft, Anne, 225
Batista, Fulgencio, 52
Bergeron, Tom, 156, 161
Boyer, Charles, 1
Brando, Marlon, 4
Brooks, Mel, 6, 9, 11, 14, 149, 222, 225, 238
Burns, George, 146

Caesar, Sid, 149
Candy, John, 146
Carson, Johnny, 116, 118, 121
Caruso, Enrico, 40, 42
Castro, Fidel, 50
Chamberlain, Richard, 180
Clinton, President Bill, xiii, 137
Clinton, Hillary, 137
Coca, Imogene, 149
Colman, Ronald, 1
Como, Perry, 79

Deacon, Richard, xii
DeLuise, Dom, 225, 238

Eddy, Nelson, 101
egg slicer, 250
Evans, Maurice, 28

Falk, Peter, 240
Fleming, Art, 220

Gilford, Jack, 95
gold money clips, 70, 75, 77, 78
Griffin, Julann, 225, 227, 229

Hamlet, 27
Hansen, Sonja, xiii
Hardy, Oliver, 168, 170, 173

Hitler, Adolph, 2
Hollywood Foreign Press, 58
hot dog, 158

Kaltenborn, H.V., xxi
Kean, Jane, 242, 245

Laurel, Stan, 168, 170, 173
Leonard, Sheldon, xii
Lindsay, Robert, 85, 146
Ludden, Allen, 29

MacArthur, Gen. Douglas, 152
MacDonald, Jeannette, 101
man feeding horse, 88
Margolin, Janet, 147
Marie, Rose, xii, 149
Martin, Steve, 144, 146, 147, 149, 210
Martinelli, Giovanni, 40, 44
McCormack, John, 106
Melvin, Allan, 33
mime, 143
Moore, Mary Tyler, xii, 60, 149, 238
Morris, Howard, 29, 149

Obama, President Barack, 137
Ode to the Buttocks Bountiful, 167

Paar, Jack, 57
Peerce, Jan, 40, 47
Pomerantz, Sol, 22, 24, 26
Radner, Gilda, 225
Randall, Tony, 120

Reiner, Annie, xiii, 86, 238
Reiner, Carl, iii, vi, vii, ix, xii, xiii, xv,
xvii, xx, xxiii, 10, 11, 14, 15, 18, 21, 22,
24, 26, 36, 60, 66, 74, 80, 82, 86, 96,
102, 109, 112, 115, 118, 122, 126, 144,
148, 149, 150, 162, 164, 174, 176, 177,
179, 186, 188, 189, 194, 196, 204, 206,
211, 212, 214, 217, 219, 222, 225, 230,
232, 235, 236, 238, 245, 246, 248, 251,
252, 254, 317, 319
Reiner, Bessie, 112
Reiner, Charles, xiii, 112, 214, 215
Reiner, Elaine, xiii
Reiner, Estelle, xiii, 164, 225, 230, 232,
235, 238, 317
Reiner, Helene, xiii
Reiner, Ilse, xiii
Reiner, Irving, 212, 215, 318
Reiner, Jake, xiii
Reiner, Livia, xiii
Reiner, Lucas, xiii, 238
Reiner, Michele, xiii
Renier, Nick, xiii
Reiner, Richard, xiii
Reiner, Rob, xiii, 238
Reiner, Romy, xiii
Rochester Summer Theater, 16
Roosevelt, President Franklin D., 98
rubber band, 72

Santoni, Reni, 147
Schwartz, Herb, 26
Segal, George, 146
Seinfeld, Jerry, xv, 121
Shakespeare, William, 138, 256
Shapiro, George, 86, 238
Silberkleit, Nicole, xiii
Simon, Neil 155
Stewart, Jimmy, 1

Tamiroff, Akim, 1
That Tumble-Down Shack
in Athlone, 104, 108
Tobias, George, 90
Tomlin, Lily, 146
Trebek, Alex, 222
Twitter, 192, 194
typewriter, 320

USO Dance Volunteers, 34

Van Dyke, Dick, xii, 33, 60, 147, 238
Vesti la Giubba, 110

White, Betty, 29, 149
Wilder, Gene, 225
Winchester, Ann, xiii
Winchester, Gordon, xiii
Winchester, Maud, xiii, 238
wooden crate, 64
Wyler, Margrit, 18

Young, Sean, 188